3x3 Basketball

CREDITS

Cover design: Hannah Park

Interior design and layout: Anja Elsen

Interior photos: Courtesy of FIBA 3x3

Managing editor: Elizabeth Evans

Copyediting: Samuel Kelly, jotortittle.com

34. A. Herrán, O. Castellano, and J. Usabiaga. "Physical Profile Comparison Between 3x3 and 5x5 Basketball Training." *Revista Internacional de Medicina y Ciencias de la Actividad Física y el Deporte* 17 (2017): 435–47.

35. "Physical Preperation of Professional 3x3 Athletes." FIBA. PDF. https://fiba3x3. basketball/docs/physical-preparation-of-professional-3x3-athletes.pdf.

36. P. G. Montgomery and B. D. Maloney. "3x3 Basketball Competition: Physical and Physiological Characteristics of Elite Players." *J Phy Fit Treatment and Sports* 5 (2018).

37. P. G. Montgomery and B. D. Maloney. "3x3 Basketball: Inertial Movement and Physiological Demands During Elite Games." *International Journal of Sports Physiology and Performance* 13 (2018): 1-20.

38. Danilo Lukić. Interview with author. June 4, 2020.

39. "Former Saint Joseph's PGs Jameer Nelson and Natasha Cloud share interest in coaching." NBC Sports. March 11, 2020. https://www.nbcsports.com/ philadelphia/76ers/jameer-nelson-natasha-cloud-st-josephs-robbie-hummel-3-x-3-usa-basketball-olympics.

40. "FIBA's newly established 3x3 Commission convene for their first meeting of the working cycle." FIBA.basketball. February 27, 2020. http://www.fiba. basketball/news/fiba%E2%80%99s-newly-established-3x3-commission-convene-for-their-first-meeting-of-the-working-cycle.

41. "A man and a vision: Basketball, more popular than soccer!" Sport Arena. April 20, 2020. https://3la3.ro/en/a-man-and-a-vision-basketball-more-popular-than-soccer_1429.html.

Luka Snoj

3x3
BASKETBALL
EVERYTHING YOU NEED TO KNOW

Foreword by Dejan Majstorović, 3-Time FIBA 3x3 World Cup Champion

Meyer & Meyer Sport

British Library Cataloguing in Publication Data
A catalogue record for this book is available from the British Library

3x3 Basketball
Maidenhead: Meyer & Meyer Sport (UK) Ltd., 2021
ISBN: 978-1-78255-226-0

© 2021 by Meyer & Meyer Sport (UK) Ltd.
Aachen, Auckland, Beirut, Dubai, Hägendorf, Hong Kong, Indianapolis, Cairo, Cape Town, Maidenhead,
Manila, New Delhi, Singapore, Sydney, Tehran, Vienna
 Member of the World Sport Publishers' Association (WSPA), www.w-s-p-a.org

Printed by: Print Consult GmbH, Munich, Germany
Printed in Slovakia

ISBN: 978-1-78255-226-0
Email: info@m-m-sports.com
www.thesportspublisher.com

CONTENTS

FOREWORD

As a player who has won multiple FIBA 3x3 World Cups, European Cups, and World Tours in the past, I am pleased and honored to write the foreword for the first-ever book about 3x3 basketball. Clearly the timing for this book is right, as 3x3 is set to make a spectacular debut on the biggest stage in sports—the Olympic Games.

3x3 is a beautiful game, and I fell in love with it from the first moment I played it. I was fortunate enough to be a part of the 3x3 community from the start, allowing me to watch this basketball discipline grow and develop to what it is today. As I helped shaped the history of 3x3, I am more excited than ever to see what the future will bring.

First, I would like to warmly congratulate Luka, who I played against in several tournaments, on his initiative in bringing together and presenting this wealth of information. Luka has been involved in 3x3 for more than a decade. As the first European player to play in the first 3x3 international professional league, he opened a door and helped pave the way for international professional players. Honestly, there weren't many of us 3x3 professional players in the past, so I am extremely happy he is the one sharing his knowledge and presenting the game to the world.

This book is one of a kind. It provides detailed insight into the game of 3x3. It is excellent, professional literature, rich with historical background, statistical data, specific terminology, strategies, game structure definitions, tips and instructions for players, and in-depth analyses. When considering all the above, clearly this book will serve as the foundation for further professional advancement in this discipline. I also hope the book will significantly contribute to the continued rise of 3x3's popularity, which currently receives less media attention than traditional basketball.

Perhaps one of the most important aspects of this book is that it shows that 3x3 and traditional basketball are not as similar as one might think. Luka has done a fantastic job systematically clarifying the differences between the two sports and explaining how 3x3 has formed its own identity. This basketball discipline is also attractive to players of traditional basketball as they can easily transition to 3x3. Luka presents and explains every facet of 3x3 basketball with clear and informative language, making this book appealing to both those who are new to the sport and those seeking further information.

It is with great pleasure that I heartily recommend this book to all who are involved in or want to be involved in the exciting and challenging world of 3x3 basketball. It is my hope and expectation that this book will be an effective learning experience and a valuable resource.

–Dejan Majstorović

3-time FIBA 3x3 World Cup Champion
4-time FIBA 3x3 World Tour Champion
2-time FIBA 3x3 Europe Cup Champion
Former number 1 player in the FIBA
3x3 World Ranking
MVP of the FIBA 3x3 World Cup 2017
MVP of the FIBA 3x3 Europe Cup 2019

INTRODUCTION

There is only one sport called basketball. But there is more to basketball than the traditional game of 5-on-5 with which most people are familiar.

3x3 basketball has not been around long as a formal and professional game, even though it has a rich origin, having been played for years on streets and playgrounds. In the past, the format of three players per side with only one basket was fondly called "21" or "three-on-three." Despite the fact 3x3 shares a lot with streetball and traditional basketball, it is important to not equate this new Olympic discipline with either one. Traditional basketball is a game of five players per side playing with two baskets. Outside of the United States, basketball has been governed by the International Basketball Federation (FIBA) since 1932. Streetball is an informal variation of basketball usually played on outdoor courts. 3x3, on the other hand, a game of three players per side using one basket, is a formal, standalone basketball discipline and was never a sub-product of the traditional game.

What makes 3x3 stand out is its inclusiveness, as it provides equal opportunities for players. This basketball discipline is by far the most accessible for all ages and backgrounds. According to FIBA, 3x3 stands for nonstop excitement and fun; 182 countries and regions participate, with almost one million registered athletes. This makes 3x3 the most popular urban team sport in the world, according to the International Olympic Committee. 3x3 is also sometimes referred to as the "10-minute sprint," so as you read this book, keep in mind that 3x3 basketball is extremely fast paced and is always played in a tournament form. At tournaments, teams never just play one game, but instead they can play a minimum of two and, in some cases, even seven or eight games in a day!

3x3 basketball has had a profound impact on my life. I fell in love with it from the beginning, probably because of the freedom it gave me to express and showcase my basketball skills and the relaxed atmosphere at events. I discovered in it something similar to the streetball I played as a kid on the playground with my friends. But my first thought was how quick and physical this discipline is.

I come from the small Central European country of Slovenia, home to just two million inhabitants, where basketball is the second most popular sport behind soccer. In Slovenia, once the basketball season ends, players usually start playing 3x3 on outdoor courts in their off-season to help develop their basketball skills. Slovenia was part of the former Yugoslavia, where basketball was extremely popular, until 1991. The Yugoslavian national team achieved impressive results on the biggest stage, winning the FIBA 1970 Basketball World Championship in my hometown of Ljubljana. Since Slovenia's independence, players like Luka Dončić Goran Dragić, Sasha Vujačić, and Radoslav Nesterović have emerged on the NBA scene and continued Slovenia's remarkable basketball legacy. However, Slovenia has also achieved stellar results in 3x3 and played a vital role in promoting and developing this game. The success has culminated in Slovenia winning medals at FIBA 3x3 World and European Cups. Slovenian teams have also been extremely successful on the FIBA 3x3 Professional Circuit, twice winning the FIBA 3x3 World Tour Final.

Maybe love of one game led me to another. Obviously, 3x3's closest relatives are traditional basketball and streetball because of the similarities they share in rules, techniques, and their common aim of scoring a basket. But I strongly believe there are significant similarities with blitz chess. When I was about seven years old, before I started playing basketball, I played chess every other day, and I eventually completed chess middle school. In blitz chess, you have a limited amount of time—maybe only five minutes per player—so you have only few seconds to think about your next move. You are constantly under time pressure, having to anticipate your opponent's strategy, react quickly, and problem solve on the fly—just like in 3x3. Once the chess match starts, the player is alone, and no help is allowed from their coach, which is also similar to 3x3, where you can't receive any coaching during the game. Both games are also played in tournament style with numerous matches a day and no time for a rest, which tests players' mental abilities. In both chess and 3x3, a side can win the game before the game clock runs out, which led me to believe that these two games have more in common than anyone previously thought.

In the early years of professional 3x3, when I also started playing it professionally overseas, people really only knew about traditional basketball. Some of them didn't know that the sport of basketball, which has been for decades one of the biggest and most popular sports in the world, has two different disciplines. Since 3x3 was not yet popular and internationally established, some people simply called it the "other" basketball game. However, in a less than a decade, 3x3 quickly developed, forged its identity, and became part of the biggest multi-sport international events. Things could really take off when it showcases at the Tokyo Olympic Games in 2021, and the afterglow could culminate in more commercial and professional opportunities.

During my career, I was never ranked as the best 3x3 player in the world; my highest world ranking was 27th. My purpose in writing this book is not to celebrate my achievements but to present the game and help people understand it. As with any new sport, understanding the fundamentals is vital before it can be properly scrutinized. Therefore, a book specifically describing every facet of the game, analyzing its principles and defining the relevant terms, is needed for people to learn and understand 3x3. One of the things that pushed and motivated me to write this book was the fact that this game was and still is relatively unknown to many and that there hasn't been widespread independent research on it.

Clearly my time researching and writing was not a sprint, but rather a marathon. Having coaching and playing experience just wasn't enough. I had to collect large amounts of data over the years, systematically study the field, research, and conduct interviews and analyses in order to properly inform, explain, and inspire readers.

On that note, I would like to thank FIBA 3x3 for providing me with previously unreleased historical, statistical, and other data that were crucial for writing this book. I also have to thank pioneering 3x3 athletes and coaches for the details shared in their interviews. I hope this book will be an inspiration to and useful literature for many players and fans of 3x3 basketball.

CHAPTER 1
INTRODUCTION TO 3X3 BASKETBALL

For the purposes of this book, we will use the official International Basketball Federation (FIBA) terminology **3x3 basketball, or **3x3** for short, which is distinct from **traditional basketball** (i.e., five-on-five).*

BASKETBALL VARIATIONS AND 3X3

Basketball is one of the world's most popular sports and people love to play it or watch it no matter what the form. There are several variations of basketball worldwide, with tweaks that differentiate it from the traditional five-on-five discipline, but the core skills that players use with and without the ball remain intact. These variations, which can be either formal or informal, look almost identical to traditional basketball, but there are differences in structure and rules. Informal basketball variations such as "streetball" are played without strict official rules, usually on the playgrounds without referees or other officials. 3x3, on the other hand, is a formal basketball discipline with strict rules. This variation involves two teams of three players each—and usually one substitute—played on one basket. The team wins if it scores 21 points first or has scored the most points by the end of the regulated time period of 10 minutes. Generally, 3x3 shares a lot in common with five-on-five basketball, including ball handling regulations and basic violation rules like goaltending, double dribble, three-second rules, and so on. 3x3 is also easily played on the half of a regular basketball court, and the fundamental skills involved in 3x3 are similar to traditional basketball. However, there are some key structural and rule differences that set the two games apart. As an example in 3x3 compared to traditional basketball, in-game coaching is not allowed; there are three players a side compared to traditional basketball's five; the 3x3 offensive shot clock is set to 12 seconds rather than basketball's 24; and 3x3 players use a unique ball which is smaller than the one used in traditional men's basketball competitions. Based on the aforementioned structural and rule differences, the gameplay of 3x3, including teams' styles and scoring preferences, also differs from basketball's, mostly because of different scoring rules. Even though a three-point arc in traditional basketball (*FIBA rules) is the same distance from the basket as the two-point arc in 3x3, 3x3 players choose to take these shots more frequently because they see more value in them. A three-pointer in traditional basketball is worth 50 percent more than a made shot inside the two-point arc, but in 3x3, a shot inside the arc is worth one point while a shot beyond the arc is worth 100 percent more: two points.

Hakeem "The Dream" Olajuwon, NBA Hall of Fame Inductee: "3×3 is the kind of game that everybody loves."[1]

Why 3x3 Was Formalized: FIBA's Goals

Before 2007, traditional basketball was FIBA's only formal and officially regulated basketball discipline. FIBA (International Basketball Federation) was founded by eight nations in 1932, and it and now brings together 213 national basketball federations worldwide. In the late 2000s, three-on-three streetball, played around the world, aroused the interest of the association. This variation was extremely popular for decades, but athletes simply didn't have an organized platform to compete more professionally. FIBA saw an excellent opportunity to change this. Their idea was to create a new discipline that would attract new athletes to basketball, allow lower-ranked basketball nations to compete, push the game of basketball into new boundaries, and increase the sport's popularity. FIBA also had a vision to make basketball the most popular sports community in the world by the 2028 Los Angeles Olympics. To attain these changes, they believed the new game format should provide entertainment, be easily accessible to players, and inexpensive and easy to organize. They believed that events should be held in iconic places, city centers, and urban areas where the action could catch the attention of passers-by.

Initially, FIBA had to overcome a few obstacles, with their first goal being to structure, organize, and formalize three-on-three. Another goal was to provide an international platform to showcase it worldwide. This led to three-on-three making its official worldwide debut in the 2010 Youth Olympic Games in Singapore. The move from three-on-three played informally on the street to a formal basketball discipline involved a name change to "3x3." In the past, 3x3 was often mistakenly referred to as "3-on-3" basketball, but FIBA has made it very clear that the official name of this basketball discipline is 3x3. The correct pronunciation FIBA has set is "3 ex 3." Since 2010, the game has quickly progressed and become global under the guidance of FIBA 3x3, which set up a World Cup and other regional cups for national teams and World Tour events for professional teams.

The popularization of 3x3 began in Europe and Asia and later spread to the USA and other parts of the world as fans fell in love with its entertainment value. 3x3 is always about more than just the on-court action. It genuinely seeks to entertain people through various side events, such as a dunking contest. The high entertainment value, urban culture, and the fact that 3x3 is organized in tournaments where spectators can see multiple games in one day has helped capture new fans who might not have been interested in hoops before.

Only seven years passed from when 3x3's first official international event was held in 2010 to when it was added to the Olympic program on June 9, 2017, slated for the 2020 Olympic Games in Tokyo. Few major sports have received such international recognition so fast. This was a result of the great work of the whole 3x3 community, most especially the cooperation of FIBA, national basketball federations, and private promotors. Many do not know who the key FIBA official was that initiated the 3x3 movement and later accelerated 3x3 development. The late FIBA Secretary General Patrick Baumann was the 3x3's early pioneer, who foresaw that it would be a major part of basketball's future. He envisioned it as a perfect game for youth because it challenges them to be more innovative. He also believed 3x3 could help expand basketball beyond traditional boundaries because costs for staging outdoor 3x3 events are lower, and not as much infrastructure is required compared to a traditional basketball game in the indoor arena. This would allow 3x3 to quickly spread to new frontiers. Furthermore, and most important, he believed that 3x3 offers non-traditional basketball countries opportunities to participate in international competitions, which can be difficult for these nations given the large number of players required to comprise a traditional basketball team. Traditional basketball tests the depth of smaller nations because teams need to have 12 players. In 3x3, however, the depth of talent is less vital because teams only need four players, putting many nations on more equal footing.

The Rise of Non-Basketball Powerhouses

This basketball discipline isn't just better balanced, but it is also more unpredictable given the short time frame and low scoring target of 21 points. There have already been many memorable underdog stories in 3x3, with Mongolia's high rankings in both the men's and women's categories a testament to this. Other countries, such as Latvia, the Netherlands, the Czech Republic, Qatar, and Ukraine have won medals in FIBA 3x3 World Cups, which was not achievable for them in traditional basketball. On the flip side, the USA—the undisputed basketball powerhouse—only won their first men's FIBA 3x3 World Cup in 2019

Men's USA team, winning their first FIBA 3x3 World Cup in 2019. From left to right: Robbie Hummel, Kareem Maddox, Canyon Barry, Damon Huffman.

and has been upstaged over the years by Eastern European countries. The red, white, and blue have had better success in the women's category, where they have won several World Cups. However, winning the first men's gold medal for the USA and getting an MVP at the 2019 FIBA 3x3 World Cup helped Robbie Hummel receive the USA Basketball Male Athlete of the Year award. The previous awardees include superstars Michael Jordan, Shaquille O'Neal, and Reggie Miller. Many high-profile NBA and WNBA players have represented the USA at FIBA 3x3 World Cups, including Zach Collins, PJ Washington, Arike Ogunbowale, and Sabrina Ionescu. This shows that even big countries have serious intentions for this up-and-coming Olympic discipline.

Team of the tournament at the FIBA 3x3 World Cup 2019: Karlis Lasmanis (LAT), Robbie Hummel (USA), Michael Hicks (POL).

Different Variations of Three Players Against Three on One Basket

Many basketball players encountered the stripped-down format of playing three against three on one basket before 3x3 was formalized. Players played this way through streetball variation on outdoor courts or at traditional basketball practices. Traditional basketball involves five players from each team at the same time on a court with two baskets, but during the course of the training process, traditional basketball coaches often reduce the number of players on the teams, with rules retained or slightly modified. This is called a small-sided basketball game and is a great way of learning basketball when it is played in the form of three against three. Some basketball federations even preferred organizing three-on-three basketball leagues for junior players, believing this format was more appropriate for young players' development, as they got more touches and playing time.

Apart from traditional five-on-five, other basketball variations were not known as official competition sports and were usually practiced outside on the street and called street basketball. They were occasionally played at amateur-level tournaments. This variation didn't have a rigid structure or a common international playing platform and wasn't formalized. It is clear that basketball players have played a format of three-on-three before, but 3x3 basketball is a formal basketball discipline with strict game rules. Another three-on-three variation is Fireball3, which is popular in the USA (the "BIG3" league). This variation has different rules from FIBA 3x3 or NBA five-on-five and is generally played inside arenas, with in-game coaching allowed and headlined by former NBA stars.

Traditional Basketball, Streetball, and 3x3 Basketball

Even though 3x3 is a standalone discipline, it has been heavily influenced by traditional basketball and streetball. The parallels are obvious, but the differences also stand out.

3x3 resembles traditional basketball and streetball in its objective of scoring more points than the opposition by shooting the ball through the hoop. It retains the same rules for dribbling and shooting, among other things. 3x3 has adopted bits of each of these formats. Its accessibility, culture, and urban nature is much closer to streetball, whereas its strict rules, structured competition platform, and professional organization is more akin to traditional basketball. Regarding playing style, 3x3 is a fusion of both, as traditional basketball is a sport of structure and discipline, while street basketball is about freedom, creativity, and spontaneous decision-making. Due to the countless similarities between basketball and 3x3, most people would think that being good in traditional basketball means being good in 3x3. This might be true to a certain degree, as skills of one game can easily translate to another. The more detailed answer to this question will be presented later, but it is important to know that having fewer players on the court, a shorter shot clock, and a smaller court size gives 3x3 an alternative style and dynamic, meaning it is played differently than traditional basketball. The gap between the two games is likely to widen over the years in terms of their playing style, rules, and specific training methods as 3x3 continues to forge its own identity.

3x3, the largest urban sport in the world, has been heavily influenced by both streetball and traditional basketball.

TRADITIONAL BASKETBALL AND ITS HISTORY

Traditional basketball is a team sport with two teams of five players, each trying to score by shooting a ball through a hoop elevated 3.05 meters (10 feet) above the ground. A successful score is called a "basket." A basket can count as one, two, or three points depending on where the shot was attempted from. The game is played on a rectangular floor, and there is a hoop at each end of the court, which is divided into two main sections by the mid-court line. It is usually played indoors in a gym. A game lasts 40 minutes by FIBA rules or 48 minutes in the NBA, and the team with the most points at the end of the game wins. Basketball is considered one of the most popular sports in the world. It arguably has the widest global reach of any sport other than football (soccer). It has become popular over the years because it's fun to watch and play, uses only simple equipment, and is an all-weather sport.

The Origins of Traditional Basketball

Dr. James Naismith invented basketball in 1891 at the YMCA in Springfield, Massachusetts. He was a physical education instructor and was determined to create an indoor, non-contact sport to keep athletes in shape throughout the winter. "Basket ball" only had 13 rules—published on January 15, 1892, in the YMCA's Triangle Magazine—and they were quite different from those of today's sport (for example, players were not allowed to dribble). The first basketball game was played with a soccer ball and two peach baskets nailed to the wall at 10-feet on a court just half the size of what we are familiar with today. Soon, basketball spread globally to Asia, Europe, South America, and all corners of the world. In 1932, FIBA was established as the international governing body for basketball, and four years later, basketball made its Olympic debut. In 1946, the most renowned basketball league, the BAA (now the NBA), was established in the USA. In the first three decades after World War II, basketball steadily grew in popularity. Interest in the game deepened because of television exposure in the 1980s, and the game's popularity exploded soon after that. With world-famous basketball players such as Earvin "Magic" Johnson, Julius Erving, Larry Bird, Michael Jordan, Allen Iverson, and Kobe Bryant, and significantly increased exposure, basketball quickly moved to the forefront of the world's sporting scene.

Triangles in Offensive Team Tactics

Traditional basketball coaches have frequently practiced three-on-three basketball to use player triangles as a basis for running tactics on offense. Cooperation between all three players is pivotal, and the movement of those players sets up good offensive options for their teammates. Basketball offensive plays such as the "UCLA offense" or the continuity basketball offense called the "triangle offense" have been popular schemes for decades, with the primary purpose of creating triangles on one side of the court in which, unlike in a two-player formation, a third player allows for more scoring options. Triangle offenses depend on a strong-side concept, creating additional scoring opportunities for players on the weak side if the defense breaks down or they decide to double-team the ball on the strong-side block. However, proper spacing is vital in the execution these offensive plays. Led by mastermind Phil Jackson, who preached the triangle offense, the Chicago Bulls (in the 1990s) and LA Lakers (in the 2000s) built traditional basketball dynasties.

Small-Sided Basketball Games

Small-sided basketball games, or games using only one basket, are abbreviated and modified versions of traditional basketball, in which players become acquainted with the key elements of basketball and systematically consolidate and improve their knowledge of the game. These games are usually played on smaller courts with fewer players and with different rules. Players nevertheless experience very similar situations to those they would encounter in traditional basketball games.[2] SSBGs are a part of most traditional basketball training programs; they have been well-researched and proven effective. According to some research, reducing the number of players increases player participation, physical demands, and the intensity of the game. It gives players more contact with the ball, leading to faster development.[3-5] Moreover, the application of these games in daily training sessions aims to optimize training time by unifying strength and conditioning with the development of technical and tactical skills.[6] For all of these reasons, traditional basketball coaches prefer SSBGs to short-duration intermittent running and other potential training methods.

Three-on-Three Small-Sided Basketball Games

Traditional basketball coaches use three-on-three SSBGs with young players to speed up their development of tactical and technical skills and their physical fitness. Coaches have also frequently used three-on-three SSBGs to develop decision-making, intentionally teaching specific situations that players encounter when competing in traditional basketball, mainly because three-player tactics are common in five-on-five offenses.

However, three-on-three SSBGs are also used for training on professional teams. In the NBA, in addition to the technical-tactical development of the players, teams use three-on-three scrimmages to rehabilitate injured players before they resume regular five-on-five practice. Three-on-three SSBGs are also used during NBA tryouts so scouts can see how well players read and understand the game. Finally, NBA teams use SSBGs as a tool for maintaining the fitness of players who don't get regular playing time.

Is Three-on-Three Basketball More Appropriate for Younger Players?

3x3 can be an excellent way to introduce youth to the sport of basketball. Some basketball leagues and national basketball federations offer 3x3 leagues for younger age groups instead of five-on-five basketball leagues, as they see this variation as more suitable for player development. Those 3x3 leagues are played concurrently with the traditional basketball season and inside the gym, with adjustments to some rules (such as a lower basket). When younger players have gained the requisite knowledge and are old enough, they transition to traditional basketball. For example, the Jr. NBA 3v3 league is available to players from 10 to 14 years old. The rules are very similar to 3x3 for senior players, with scoring and foul rules retained. The league's objective is to impact young players' long-term development by delivering a fun on-court experiences that creates opportunities for boys and girls to engage in play, foster skill development, and cultivate friendships. Many indicators show that 3x3 basketball might be a more appropriate format for young (13 years or younger) or inexperienced players compared to traditional basketball, as it allows a higher number of effective possessions.[7-8] Moreover, traditional basketball rosters are comprised of 12 players, meaning some players will rarely step foot on the court. In 3x3, there are only four players on a team, and they all receive a fair chunk of game time. It's hard to determine whether one discipline is more appropriate than another because it depends on a player's preference, ability, potential, and other factors. However, 3x3 can be a great way to train for basketball at a young age, as it promotes position-less basketball, allowing young players to develop a versatile skill set. When looking to participate at youth events, younger players should not forget that the first rule of basketball is to enjoy playing—winning should not be prioritized.

Table 1: Fundamental advantages of 3x3 and three-on-three SSBGs for younger basketball players[2, 7–9]

Allows more touches on the ball	Less complex tactics	More relative playing time
Develops toughness	Involves all players more evenly	Develops one-on-one game
Develops a versatile skill set	Increases a player's on-court responsibility	Develops quick thinking

Julius Randle, NBA player:

"It [3x3] is a lot different than five-on-five. ... The spacing is different, the movement and all that type of stuff is different, so it gives you a lot more freedom. It gives you little bit more ability to work on your game. You learn how to move without the ball, you learn how to space correctly and adjust to that. It's good."[10]

Basketball Players and 3x3

Many superstar basketball players learned important skills and built their knowledge by playing 3x3 during their formative years. 3x3 has really only touched the ground, but it has already shaped basketball players such as Sabrina Ionescu, who is the NCAA all-time leader in triple doubles and the only NCAA Division I female basketball player to record 2,000 points, 1,000 assists, and 1,000 rebounds in a career. She has played in multiple 3x3 events, won the USA's 3x3 national championship, and been drafted as the number-one pick of the 2020 WNBA draft. In 2021, Charli Collier become the sixth WNBA number-one draft pick with 3x3 experience, and Paige Bueckers will probably continue this extraordinary series in the future as she is currently dominating women's college basketball. Moreover, other young male prospects who played in official 3x3 events in their youth got drafted in the 2020 NBA draft, such as Payton Pritchard, Theo Maledon, and Leandro Bolmaro. To better understand how can 3x3 help a young athlete, reflections of other well-known basketball players who have played in official FIBA 3x3 competitions are presented in the following pages.

3X3 BASKETBALL ★

Table 2:   Notable male basketball players who competed in official
3x3 competitions in their youth

Player	League
Zach Collins	NBA
PJ Washington	NBA
Jae'Sean Tate	NBA
Rondae Hollis-Jefferson	NBA
Payton Pritchard	NBA
Theo Maledon	NBA
Alfonzo McKinnie	NBA
Sekou Doumbouya	NBA
Gabriel Deck	NBA
Usman Garuba	Liga ACB
Mikhail Andreyevich Kulagin	VTB United League

*NBA – Premier professional basketball league in the world
*Liga ACB – Top Spanish basketball league
*VTB United League – International / Top Russian basketball league

Zach Collins, NBA player:

"It [3x3] kind of helped me grow a little bit too, both as a basketball player and as a man, so it was a very positive experience. It was tough at the beginning; I definitely struggled when I started playing 3x3. But I got used to it progressively, but it's different from basketball. The game is fast, you never have breaks, and you keep playing without stopping. It's very intense, but I really like it."[11]

Rondae Hollis-Jefferson, NBA player:

"I learned a lot about my game, worked on my basketball IQ and also on how to play with some international rules. I really enjoyed it, and those international experiences were very positive and constructive for me, both on a human level and basketball wise."[12]

Alfonzo McKinnie, NBA player:

"I think 3x3 has helped me grow as a leader. 3x3 also helped me with my one-on-one skill set."[13]

Alfonzo McKinnie (USA) in action at the FIBA 3x3 World Cup 2016.

Alfonzo McKinnie, giving an interview at the FIBA 3x3 World Cup 2016 for the USA.

Table 3:   Notable female basketball players who competed in official
            3x3 competitions in their youth

Player	League
Sabrina Ionescu	WNBA
Chiney Ogwumike	WNBA
Jewell Lloyd	WNBA
Skylar Diggins-Smith	WNBA
A'ja Wilson*	WNBA
Satou Sabally	WNBA
Charli Collier**	WNBA
Arike Ogunbowale	WNBA
Astou Ndur	WNBA
Paige Bueckers	NCAA

WNBA – Top women's basketball league in the USA
NCAA – National Collegiate Athletic Association
*She was the 2020 WNBA MVP.
**She was the 2021 WNBA number-one draft pick.

Sabrina Ionescu, number-one pick of the 2020 WNBA draft:

"3x3 is beneficial, and it helps us get tougher...You have to play through contact... You can't rely on a coach or anyone else to call plays or tell you what to do, because you have 12 seconds. Honestly, I think it makes you take your game to another level and take it out of your comfort zone and take ownership and leadership...I enjoy 3x3."[14]

Sabrina Ionescu (USA) at the FIBA 3x3 World Cup 2018.

On the other hand, famous basketball players such as Dennis Schröder, Jorge Garbajosa, Robbie Hummel, and Anton Ponkrashov have tried their luck in 3x3 during or after their professional basketball careers. Initially, they were surprised at how different 3x3 is to traditional basketball.

Anton Ponkrashov, Olympic silver medalist:

"It was a big surprise for me. ... On the first match, after three minutes, I thought 'easy game.' After six minutes, I was so tired I realized I wasn't ready for that. After three games, I was dead."[15]

Jorge Garbajosa, ex-NBA player and FIBA World Cup gold medalist:

"It's such a different sport than basketball. It requires different skills and gives more one-on-one opportunities."[16]

STREETBALL AND ITS HISTORY

Streetball is an informal and unique variation of basketball that can be played in different forms. It is typically played on outdoor courts, especially in urban areas without fixed rules, and mostly as a pick-up game. Most professional basketball players have played streetball at some time in their lives. It helps improve a player's fitness and basketball skill set and allows players to have fun playing basketball off-season.

Streetball was first played on the streets of major cities in the United States—hence its name. Its specific origin is unclear, but it's believed to have been played in backyards and playgrounds since basketball started. Every city where streetball has been played has its own unique culture, flair, and rules. The most well-known location for streetball is Rucker Park in Harlem, New York, which is considered the mecca of streetball. In 1946, a New York City Department of Parks employee named Holcombe Rucker began to organize a summer tournament for neighborhood kids. Thus, the summer streetball league was born. Until that time, streetball had belonged to the streets and was strictly an unofficial game. Later, in the 60s and 70s, Joe "The Destroyer" Hammond, Earl "The Goat" Manigault, and other players became famous for playing streetball in New York.[17] Streetball and traditional basketball were similar, but never quite the same, with differing rules. Being good at one didn't necessarily mean being good at the other.

What bridged the gap between streetball and traditional basketball was the emergence of famous NBA stars playing streetball during their summer off-season. Some of the best NBA players from the 1970s and 80s, like Wilt Chamberlain, Nate Archibald, Kareem Abdul-Jabbar, and Julius Erving, were regulars on the streetball courts of New York. Amateur streetballers had no fear playing alongside the pros; in fact, they relished the opportunity. In the 2000s, the And1 Mixtapes and NBA superstars such as Kobe Bryant, Vince Carter, and Allen Iverson gave public exposure to streetball.[17] Meanwhile, other well-known NBA players, supported by hip-hop artists such as Jay-Z, played in streetball tournaments all over the USA during the summer. Streetball tournaments in various formats had been organized around the world for decades: one-on-one (King of the Rock), three-on-three (Gus Macker 3-on-3, Hoop It Up, Somecity), or five-on-five (Quai 54, Venice Basketball League, Sunset Dongdan).

Streetball vs. Basketball

Both streetball and traditional basketball have heavily influenced 3x3 well beyond its rules and style of play. They both inspired aspiration to victory and promotion of a healthy lifestyle. However, streetball developed its own urban culture and took a relaxed approach to basketball, prioritizing style and entertainment value. Traditional basketball heavily emphasizes team play and the correct use of an individual player in the system, whereas in streetball, individual skill with the ball and speed tend to come out on top.

Streetball has several other notable differences from traditional basketball:

★ Streetball is not formalized, and rules are not strictly standardized.

★ Streetball's style of play is a lot more improvisational, aggressive, and physical.

★ Streetball is played on outside courts, mostly on asphalt.

★ Streetball typically does not use player positions, while traditional basketball does.

★ Streetball pick-up games have no referees, and players self-call the fouls. Therefore, fouls, travels, and double dribbles are rarely called.

★ Streetball games are played in different formats, such as five-on-five, one-on-one, or three-on-three.

★ Streetball doesn't have the same structured playing platform as traditional basketball and doesn't have representation by a national federation or governing body.

Julius Erving, NBA champion and MVP:

"I grew up playing playground basketball. When you got on, whether you were the first one there in the park in the morning or whether somebody lost and you got on, you tried to stay on for the duration of the day."[18]

Three-on-Three Streetball With One Basket

Three-on-three streetball with one basket, also called "twenty-one," is 3x3's "predecessor" and one of the most popular and common variations of streetball. It has its own unofficial rules that vary from one place to another. For athletes, this game is a way of showcasing their talent to the neighborhood. One simply has to find an outdoor basketball court. Prior to the game, the players determine the rules, and it is highly likely that it will be the first and only time the team will ever play together. The popularity of this streetball variation gained the attention of FIBA and consequently led to formation of a new formal basketball discipline—3x3.

LaMelo Ball, youngest player in NBA history to record a triple-double, on why he is such a good rebounder:

"I played a lot of 21 growing up so it's just a whole lot of basketball. It's pretty much just instinct, I guess."[19]

FIBA 3x3's famous motto: From the streets to the Olympics.

CHAPTER 2
THE RISE OF 3X3 AND ITS HISTORY

3X3'S HISTORY AND EARLY BEGINNINGS

While traditional basketball has had its own international governing body since 1932, streetball has never had one. Three-on-three streetball tournaments have always been organized by private promoters; streetball, as an informal type of basketball, has never been organized or formalized like traditional basketball.

But in the late 2000s, FIBA came up with an accessible form of basketball in which players, teams, and nations could compete on a structured and organized platform. This idea would revolutionize three-on-three basketball and turn it into a global craze. FIBA's philosophy, the brainchild of General Secretary Patrick Baumann, was to put a framework around the streetball tournaments played around the world. As part of its grand vision to make basketball the world's most popular sport, FIBA embraced 3x3 to further promote, unite, and develop the game. Ever since its genesis, 3x3 has been intended to be an innovative catalyst and accelerator to the development of basketball worldwide as well as a new basketball discipline that appeals to young people. No longer would fans travel to suburban indoor arenas, since basketball would be brought straight into the hearts of cities. With showmanship on the court, iconic cityscape backdrops, non-stop music, and the best street artists, the new basketball discipline would turn into a genuine urban culture festival.

FIBA's first goal was to provide a clear set of rules and to better formalize three-on-three so that players, teams, and nations could compete on a more structured platform. FIBA also wanted to retain basketball players, most notably safeguarding teenagers drifting away from the sport, and offer them a different basketball format with a chance of representing their nations at the international level. This aligned perfectly with FIBA's initial mission, "everybody can be successful with 3x3," which was to enable lower-ranked basketball nations and those countries with smaller sport-related budgets to attain international recognition through this new exciting basketball discipline.

Most important, 3x3 represented a perfect example of a low-cost, high-quality event as it was less expensive, more accessible, and easier to organize and compete in compared to traditional basketball, making it highly attractive for both players and organizers. Clearly embracing an additional basketball discipline has had numerous advantages, but, more importantly, it provided more global reach as it pushed the sport of basketball into new frontiers. Consequentially, this led to more career opportunities and brought new people to basketball.

Horacio Muratore, former FIBA president:

"The intensity and skill level of the 3x3 game is such that there are no traditional 3x3 powerhouses, and new countries have emerged since the first YOG experience in 2010. This was our main objective back in 2007."[20]

2007–2009

In 2007, FIBA established the first official rules for three-on-three basketball and then intensified its efforts under a project titled FIBA 33. The dedicated three-on-three project consisted of a group of FIBA employees solely focused on creating rules and a structured platform for players, managing the first test events and organizing further international tournaments. FIBA conducted surveys to gauge their new product. Following the first few tests, they tinkered with the rules before and after the 2007 Asian Indoor Games in Macau, where "3on3 basketball game" was presented as a demonstration sport. Further test events around the world were held, such as at the Asian Beach Games in October 2008 and the Asian Youth Games the following year. Although a global sports event was so-far lacking, in December 2007 the IOC decided to include three-on-three basketball in the 2010 Youth Olympic Games (YOG), which would be three-on-three basketball's international debut. The YOG did not include traditional basketball, so three-on-three was the sport's representative, chosen because of it had a youthful and positive image, along with being an adaptable game through its simple infrastructure and equipment. In the lead-up to the YOG, FIBA worked intensively on a standard set of rules for three-on-three basketball while also examining the possibility of organizing further international events and setting up a yearly competition calendar.

2010

In 2010, a set of objectives and recommendations from a FIBA 33 working group were adopted to form a roadmap for the further development of three-on-three basketball. This included an improved set of rules, a proposition for a unique technology-driven strategy centered on a worldwide network of competitions, and an online community of players. The online community, called 3x3 planet, would bring the players together and enable them to search and apply for tournaments worldwide. Event participation and performances would also result in an individual world ranking.

In September 2010, the FIBA World Congress in Istanbul was provided with an in-depth presentation on the discipline and FIBA's ambitions for the further development of three-on-three basketball, which included its becoming an Olympic sport. A specialized FIBA department was then established and moved to FIBA's headquarters under the leadership of President Yvan Mainini and Secretary-General Patrick Baumann. FIBA 33 as a development project ended, and three-on-three basketball became institutionalized. It now had an international governing body (FIBA 3x3) and was slickly rebranded as 3x3. Led by Baumann, 3x3 was rejuvenated through new rules, a new structure with its own regular competitions, and an international playing platform, which fueled its rapid development worldwide. They successfully persuaded streetball organizers to try 3x3 and its new rules.

Stephon Marbury, former NBA player and CBA league champion:

"3x3 is super dope. Now you're governing basketball as a whole. You are not leaving anything or anyone out. You are covering all bases."[21]

The First Official International Event

The first Youth Olympic Games, an international multi-sport event for young athletes up to 18 years old, were held in Singapore in August 2010. 3x3 was labelled as the "hottest ticket in town" and showed plenty of promise. The 3x3 tournament featured 20 national teams in both the men's and women's categories. The men's gold medal match saw Serbia beat Croatia (22-9), while China won gold against Australia (33-29) in the women's. 3x3's international debut was a great success and praised by players, coaches, fans, and the media.

Patrick Baumann, former FIBA secretary general:

"[3x3 is] not an alternative, but it's an add-on, and we may have it at the Olympics as early as 2020. For many people around the world, playing 3-on-3 is their introduction to basketball. The Youth Olympic Games is the first step, then we will probably have a World Cup and Masters series starting in two years. Then you create a generation of professional players."[22]

Vlade Divac, ex-NBA player and ex-NBA GM, on YOG 2010:

"I talked to the kids, and they enjoyed it very much, and it looks like the fans are also enjoying it, so it is very important to spread this sport around the world."[23]

2011

On March 13, 2011, FIBA's central board approved the roadmap proposed by FIBA 3x3 during a meeting in Lyon, and the go-ahead resulted in a test phase held over the European summer, which included a fact-finding mission during numerous events. The first-ever official FIBA 3x3 international tournament was the U18 3x3 World Cup in Italy on September 9, 2011. Teams from 60 countries took part in the tournament—36 in the men's competition and 24 in women's.

In August, FIBA officially unveiled the logo for 3x3 basketball, and the final basic pieces for the 3x3's future were set in December with FIBA's central board giving a further green light to an international competition calendar for 2012, which included the establishment of the 3x3 Professional Circuit and the first FIBA 3x3 World Cup. FIBA 3x3's vision for 3x3 to be a professional basketball discipline became a reality in 2012 when the FIBA 3x3 Pro Circuit was established in an effort to ensure players could earn a living.

As 3x3 was gaining momentum each year, more and more national federations were starting to adopt it. These national basketball federations, including those in Denmark, Spain, France, Slovenia, Serbia, Switzerland, and Lithuania, followed FIBA 3x3's lead and dedicated their resources to 3x3, anticipating the sport's global growth. They employed professionals within their federations oversee 3x3 development and coaches for 3x3 national teams. National federations also started organizing 3x3 single-event championships and national tours. In some countries, private promoters set up grassroots 3x3 tournaments and tours showcasing the new rules as part of FIBA 3x3's global push. Now recognized internationally, 3x3 was on a trajectory to be part of the world's biggest sporting events.

2012

In June 2012, FIBA 3x3 rolled out the internet platform 3x3planet—later renamed play.fiba3x3.com. This important and easily accessible online platform represents the largest sports community in the world through a network of hundreds of organizers, thousands of tournaments, and millions of players. It interconnected all users and was easily accessible to all. Most important, a player-centered digital platform and repository for 3x3 games created an individual 3x3 world ranking, which indirectly lead to the calculation of a 3x3 team ranking and 3x3 federation ranking. Through this online platform, 3x3 players of all categories and levels worldwide could register for free, search for events, and apply to participate in tournaments in their appropriate category.

Later that year, the FIBA 3x3 World Tour, which followed the Pro Circuit format, started with men's professional events held in several cities all over the world. Its professionalization was established by prize pools for the best teams in each tournament. In August, the first-ever FIBA 3x3 World Cup was held and staged in Athens, featuring men's, women's, and mixed competitions. There were no qualifications for the World Cup, as FIBA 3x3 wanted to invite as many federations as possible to participate in an effort to widely showcase the game.

Patrick Baumann, former FIBA secretary general:

"The launch of 3x3planet.com represents a major milestone in the development of 3x3 basketball. It makes organizing and playing basketball simpler and more accessible, giving millions of players the opportunity to be part of a worldwide community. 3x3planet.com is something every 3x3 player needs to be a part of."[24]

First FIBA 3x3 World Cup in Athens, Greece.

3X3 BASKETBALL ★

Timeline:
3x3's Debut at International Sporting Events
and the Founding of Standalone Competitions

August 15, 2010: 3x3's first official international event, YOG 2010.

September 9, 2011: FIBA 3x3's first official international event, the 3x3 U18 World Cup.

July 11, 2012: World University 3x3 Championship (FISU).

July 14, 2012: FIBA 3x3 Pro Circuit.

August 23, 2012: FIBA 3x3 World Cup.

May 15, 2013: FIBA 3x3 Asia Cup.

May 23, 2014: ISF 3x3 Basketball World School Championship.

September 5, 2014: FIBA 3x3 Europe Cup.

June 23, 2015: European Games.

June 4, 2017: FIBA 3x3 U23 Nations League.

November 3, 2017: FIBA 3x3 Africa Cup.

June 1, 2018: South American Games.

June 27, 2018: Mediterranean Games.

July 26, 2018: Central American and Caribbean Games.

August 21, 2018: Asian Games 2018.

October 3, 2018: FIBA 3x3 U23 World Cup.

May 31, 2019: FIBA3x3 Women Series.

July 18, 2019: Pacific Games.

July 27, 2019: Pan American Games.

August 21, 2019: African Games.

August 13, 2019: ANOC World Beach Games.

Not Yet Played:

1. Commonwealth Games

In August 2017, it was announced that 3x3 would be part of the 2022 Commonwealth Games in Birmingham, England.

2. Olympic Games

3x3 will debut at the Tokyo Olympic Games in 2021, as the Games were postponed in 2020 because of the Covid-19 pandemic.

From 2013 Onward

In August 2014, under the leadership of newly elected FIBA President Horacio Muratore, the FIBA Central Board defined the four strategic pillars as the key areas of focus and work during the 2014-2019 cycle. The mission of those strategic pillars was to increase sports participation, unify the community, as well as further promote and develop the sport of basketball. Not surprisingly, due to its recent success, 3x3 basketball represented one of the four pillars. Later FIBA 3x3 strived to further the development of professional teams. This is reflected in the growth in the number of competitions and the prize pool. It all culminated in the most momentous occasion on June 9, 2017, when 3x3 was granted Olympic status and proposed to debut at the 2020 Summer Olympic Games. Nearly 90 years after basketball was first played at Summer Olympics in Berlin. This recognition has provided 3x3 with global legitimacy and increased the status of its brand.

LeBron James, NBA superstar:

"I think it's great for basketball. For us to be able to add another category to the Olympics, another basketball category, I think it's pretty great."[25]

Patrick Baumann, former FIBA secretary general:

"This is a historic day for FIBA and 3x3 basketball. It is the recognition of 10 years of hard work to codify the rules of 3x3 and to innovate with a unique 3x3 digital platform and player ranking system that bring together athletes with private and institutional organizers in a worldwide network of FIBA-organized or sanctioned 3x3 events."[20]

Jim Tooley, USA Basketball CEO:

"USA Basketball is excited that 3x3 basketball has been added to 2020 Olympic Games. It's a popular and growing sports; it's nonstop; it's fast-paced; high energy; and an exciting version of the game."[26]

THE 3X3 COMPETITION SYSTEM

A 3x3 competition is always played in tournament style either as a single standalone event or as part of a series in different formats, such as leagues, Quests, and tours. A 3x3 tournament offers multiple games per day, which sharply contrasts with traditional basketball's competition system. Basketball fans might be used to a league system or the NBA playoff system, where the first team to win four games wins the series. It's more cutthroat in 3x3, which has single-game elimination in the knockout phase, fueling more upsets. The NCAA Division I Men's Basketball Tournament, famously called "March Madness," is also organized as a single-elimination tournament. However, in March Madness, teams play only once per day, whereas 3x3 teams always play multiple games a day and up to six or seven a day in grassroots tournaments.

Players need to be in great shape in order to keep up with 3x3's competition system, which includes playing multiple games in one day.

Who Is an Organizer and for Whom Are Events Organized?

3x3 events can be organized by FIBA 3x3, national federations or private organizers. But for whom can those competitions be organized?

First, 3x3 competitions can be organized for professional teams. Those teams can compete in privately organized professional leagues or on the FIBA 3x3 Pro Circuit, where they represent cities. Second, international competitions can be organized for national teams. And third, competitions can be organized for any other team—grassroots events that are open to all teams, all ages, and all skill levels. The best 3x3 players usually take part in multiple levels of competition, playing on the FIBA 3x3 Pro Circuit, in private professional leagues, in national championships, at grassroots events, and to represent their national teams at international competitions, all within same season.

Types of 3x3 Tournaments

Top-level tournaments are usually held at a single venue, outdoors, with one 3x3 court at their disposal. A 3x3 tournament comprises a series of games which are played either on one day or spread out over multiple days, and the teams compete for an overall prize. 3x3's trademark classic format is round robins in a group stage followed by a single-elimination knockout phase, leading to a final game.

Seeding Rules at the FIBA 3x3 Events

Before the tournament starts, competitors are seeded into multiple groups at the first stage, where they play in a round-robin system. Teams at official FIBA 3x3 events are seeded based on the 3x3 team's world ranking on the aggregate of ranking points of the three highest ranked players of each team and then placed in pools based on their seed number, while teams in grassroots events can be also seeded randomly. When an organizer is using a 3x3 team world ranking for seeding, the presumption is that the lower-ranked teams will play in the first stages of the tournaments while the higher-ranked teams make it to the elimination stage.

The Hierarchy of the FIBA 3x3 Competition Network

The FIBA 3x3 competition network is a hierarchy system providing a carrot for teams in lower-level events, who can then progress to higher tiers. The structure of the worldwide 3x3 competition network—composed of all FIBA-endorsed 3x3 events—is divided into 10 color-coded competition levels. The top-level event is the World Tour, which is played by professional 3x3 teams. All events operate under the same in-court rules and off-court regulations, creating an interconnected competition pyramid. A team might get together for a local recreational event but soon enough—in the spirit of the game's motto, "from the streets to the world stage"—find themselves competing as professionals on the FIBA 3x3 World Tour. For an event to be considered a part of the competition network, it has to be FIBA 3x3 endorsed. Any event can be FIBA 3x3 endorsed if it uses FIBA 3x3 rules, using

EventMaker for management of the tournament, uploading the results, and ensuring all participating players are registered on play.fiba3x3.com. However, it is up to the basketball federation or private organizer to decide which category and type of competition they will offer to contestants at a grassroots-level event. Contrastingly, FIBA 3x3 organizes official competitions of fixed types and in fixed categories.

Levels and Classification of 3x3 Events

3x3 events in the FIBA 3x3 hierarchy competition network are classified based on the level of the competition, with top tier events generating more world ranking points for players. The FIBA 3x3 World Tour is the highest-level event, followed by Challengers and FIBA 3x3 Cups, such as the FIBA 3x3 World Cup. High-level events consequently attract more high-ranked teams. This ensures that players travel worldwide to participate in tournaments in order to be invited to the next showpiece events. Another advantage of being higher ranked, of course, is that those teams get pole positions at events as the top seeds. This might lead to playing "easier" opponents in the group phase.

Event Level		Endorsed	Pro Events	National-team**
· Black	10		· World Tour	
· Red	9		· Challengers	· FIBA Cups (incl. U23)
· Pink	8	· Super Quest	· Women's Series	· FIBA U23 Nations League
· Brown	7	· Quest final		· FIBA U18 Cups
· Purple	6	· Quest stops · Lite Quest final		
· Blue	5	· Lite Quest stops		
· Olive	4	· All other open		
· Green	3	· 40+ and U18		
· Orange	2			
· Yellow	1	· U15		
· White	0	· U13		

** FIBA 3x3 Official National Team Competitions

Event Level is a coding displayed with colors and numbered from 10 to 1, signaling the hierarchy of events in the competition network.

FIBA 3X3 ENDORSED EVENTS

Definitions:

★ **Pro Circuit:** All men's Pro Circuit events and all FIBA 3x3 women's series events.

★ **Pro Event:** One or more Challengers, WT events, or FIBA 3x3 Women's Series events.

★ **Pro Qualifiers:** A competition to qualify for a men's Pro Event. There are three kinds of Pro Qualifiers:
  − Lite Quest
  − Quest
  − Super Quest

★ **Wild Card:** Invitation to play in a pro event.

★ **FIBA 3x3 World Tour:** A FIBA 3x3 official competition for men consisting of a series of WT Masters and one WT Final.

★ **World Tour Qualifier:** A 3x3 competition which qualifies at least one team to one WT Masters.

1 Men's Pro Circuit

The men's Pro Circuit, which began in 2012, consists of a series of Challengers and World Tour Masters and culminates in the showpiece World Tour Final. Any group of four players from any nation can take part in lower-level tournaments and, if successful, then qualify for the World Tour. Players are free to form teams but can't play for two different validated teams in men's pro events in the same season. As a rule, the name of a validated team represents the team's city's name and determines their country. World Tour and Challenger events are run over two days, where 12 teams compete in the main draw in round robins made up of four groups of three teams. The top two teams from each group qualify for the single-elimination knockout phase. Most importantly, players in World Tour and Challenger events earn prize money based on their final standings in each event.

Table 4:   Players with the most won events on the FIBA3x3 Pro Circuit
            prior to the 2021 season

Ranking	Name	Surname	Team	Events Won
1	Marko	Savić	Novi Sad (SRB)	33
2	Dejan	Majstorović	Novi Sad (SRB)	32
3	Dušan	Domović Bulut	Novi Sad (SRB)	31

2   World Tour (Level 10)

The FIBA 3x3 World Tour is the most prestigious men's competition and pinnacle event of the open network of FIBA-endorsed 3x3 tournaments. It is the backbone of the 3x3 basketball. One World Tour season consists of multiple World Tour events (Masters) and concludes with the World Tour Final. Due to the Covid-19 pandemic, the 2020 World Tour season was shortened, but the 2019 season consisted of 228 games, 11 World Tour Masters, and concluded with the World Tour Final in Utsunomiya, Japan. Teams can qualify for the World Tour Masters through FIBA-designated WT Qualifiers (which may either be Challengers, Quests, or Super Quests), by automatic allocation as hard-seeded teams, or through wildcard selection.

Prior to the 2021 Pro Circuit season, 69 World Tour events have been played. World Tour series have been hosted by 28 different cities across 19 countries, underlining the global spread of 3x3. Several 3x3 teams from various countries have won World Tour events. The most successful country on the World Tour prior to the 2021 season is the United Arab Emirates with 15 World Tour event wins. This is due to the dominance of 3x3 superstar team Novi Sad Al Wahda. The UAE is followed by Serbia, Slovenia, and the United States of America.

World Tour in Doha, Qatar.

World Tour in Saskatoon, Canada.

Adam Silver, NBA commissioner, at World Tour Lausanne 2016:

"I love basketball no matter how it is played. 3x3 played in this fashion is incredibly exciting. The games are short and highly competitive. I just think it is fantastic."[27]

Table 5:   FIBA 3x3 World Tour champions

Season	Team	Country
2012	San Juan	Puerto Rico
2013	Brezovica	Slovenia
2014	Novi Sad	Serbia
2015	Novi Sad Al Wahda	UAE
2016	Ljubljana	Slovenia
2017	Zemun	Serbia
2018	Novi Sad Al Wahda	UAE
2019	Novi Sad	Serbia
2020	Riga	Latvia

3x3 BASKETBALL ★

Table 6:   FIBA 3x3 World Tour most valuable player

Season	Player name	Team
2015	Dušan Domović Bulut	Novi Sad Al Wahda (UAE)
2016	Jasmin Hercegovac	Ljubljana (SLO)
2017	Stefan Stojačić	Liman (SRB)
2018	Dušan Domović Bulut	Novi Sad Al Wahda (UAE)
2019	Dominique Jones	NY Harlem (USA)
2020	Nauris Miezis	Riga (LAT)

Table 7:   FIBA 3x3 World Tour most spectacular player

Season	Player name	Team
2015	Terrence Romeo	Manilla West (PH)
2016	Dušan Domović Bulut	Novi Sad Al Wahda (UAE)
2017	Dušan Domović Bulut	Novi Sad Al Wahda (UAE)
2018	Dušan Domović Bulut	Novi Sad Al Wahda (UAE)
2019	Dušan Domović Bulut	Novi Sad (SRB)
2020	Ignas Vaitkus	Utena (LT)

3x3 Novi Sad, the most successful team in World Tour history.

Dušan Domović Bulut.

3X3 BASKETBALL ★

Table 8: Highest points-per-game average by a player with more than 10 games on the FIBA 3x3 World Tour prior to the 2020 season

Ranking	Name	Surname	Country	Points per game
1	Michael	Hicks	Poland	9.35
2	Željko	Palavra	BiH	8.89
3	Chris	Reaves	USA	8.92
4	Catalin	Vlaicu	Romania	7.84
5	Terrence Bill	Romeo	Philippines	7.67
6	Dušan	Domović Bulut	Serbia	7.48
7	Ovidijus	Varanauskas	Lithuania	7.23
8	Rodrigo Diguinho	Del'arco	Brazil	7.19
9	Dominique Victor	Jones	USA	7.04
10	Karlis	Lasmanis	Latvia	6.93

3   Challenger (Level 9)

FIBA 3x3 Challenger is a premium World Tour qualifier comprised of a standalone, international tournament with prize money. Teams can qualify to the Challenger through FIBA-designated Lite Quest, automated allocation based on team ranking, or as a wildcard.

4   Super Quest (Level 8)

A 3x3 Super Quest is an international, standalone, invitational tournament that follows specific regulations. Teams from at least three different countries compete in the Super Quest, but only two teams will then qualify for a WT Masters.

5   Quest Final (Level 7)

3x3 Quest is part of the FIBA 3x3 competition network and, if selected by FIBA, it may serve as a qualifier for a WT Masters Qualification Draw. It can be

★   a competition of at least three interconnected tournaments with a minimum 150 participating teams in all categories and tournaments and with open registration rules, or

★   a competition that follows specific regulations and pays, on average per tournament, the same as prize money from a Super Quest.

Individual basketball associations or other private organizers set up Quests each season. Since it consists of more than one stop, only the Quest Final (Level 7) sends the teams to the World Tour Master. The best examples of Quests are national championship leagues or tours. Other professional leagues organized by either national associations or private organizers also represent Quests. Thus, players can first play in a "private" professional league and then also compete on the FIBA 3x3 Pro Circuit. When they play on the World Tour, their World ranking can quickly rise.

6   The FIBA 3x3 Women's Series (Level 8)

The Women's Series is the first-ever FIBA 3x3 competition dedicated to women, launched in 2019. It is similar to the World Tour, but teams represent their national federations. France became the first Women's Series champion in 2019.

THE MOST PROMINENT FIBA 3X3 EVENTS FOR NATIONAL TEAMS

1   The FIBA 3x3 World Cup

Serbia dominated the men's 3x3 World Cup for years until the USA won their first gold medal in 2019. Men's and women's events have always been played concurrently because FIBA 3x3 strives for gender parity. The FIBA 3x3 World Cup was held every second year until 2016, when it became an annual marquee event. However, due to the Covid-19 pandemic, the 2020 World Cup was suspended.

Table 9:   World Cup medalists in the men's category

Year	1st	2nd	3rd
2012	Serbia	France	Ukraine
2014	Qatar	Serbia	Russia
2016	Serbia	USA	Slovenia
2017	Serbia	Netherlands	Ukraine
2018	Serbia	Netherlands	Slovenia
2019	USA	Latvia	Poland

The Serbia men's team and the USA women's team were gold medalists at FIBA 3x3 World Cup 2012.

At FIBA 3x3 World Cup 2017, Serbia's men's team and Russia's women's team were gold medalists.

3X3 BASKETBALL ★

Table 10: World Cup medalists in the women's category

Year	1st	2nd	3rd
2012	USA	France	Australia
2014	USA	Russia	Belgium
2016	Czech Republic	Ukraine	USA
2017	Russia	Hungary	Netherlands
2018	Italy	Russia	France
2019	China	Hungary	France

At the FIBA 3x3 World Cup 2019, Serbia's men's team and Russia's women's team won gold medals.

Table 11: Highest point-per-game average in the men's category at the FIBA 3x3 World Cup prior to the 2021 season

Ranking	Name	Surname	Country	Points per game
1	Michael	Hicks	Poland	8.79
2	Davi	Rossetto	Brazil	8.60
3	Paulius	Beliavicius	Lithuania	8.00
4	Karlis	Lasmanis	Latvia	7.58
5	Gionata	Zampolli	Italy	7.50
6	Tom	Wright	Australia	7.25
7	Gabriel	Deck	Argentina	7.20
8	Duje	Kaliterna	Croatia	7.18
9	Jan	Stehlík	Czech Republic	7.14
10	Mychael	Henry	USA	7.14

Table 12: Highest point-per-game average in women's category at the FIBA 3x3 World Cup prior to the 2021 season

Ranking	Name	Surname	Country	Points per game
1	Houda	Hamrouni	Tunisia	7.60
2	Jewell	Loyd	USA	7.33
3	Ganna	Rulyova	Ukraine	7.29
4	Bettina	Bozóki	Hungary	7.08
5	Petra	Szabo	Hungary	7.00

Michael Hicks is the player with the highest points per game average in both the World Tour and the World Cup.

World Cups always attract big crowds.

2   The FIBA 3x3 Europe Cup

Table 13: FIBA 3x3 Europe Cup medalists in men's category

Year	1st	2nd	3rd
2014	Romania	Slovenia	Lithuania
2016	Slovenia	Serbia	Netherlands
2017	Latvia	Slovenia	Ukraine
2018	Serbia	Latvia	Slovenia
2019	Serbia	France	Lithuania

Table 14: FIBA 3x3 Europe Cup medalists in women's category

Year	1st	2nd	3rd
2014	Russia	Slovenia	Belgium
2016	Hungary	Romania	Russia
2017	Russia	Spain	Netherlands
2018	France	Netherlands	Ukraine
2019	France	Spain	Latvia

3   The FIBA 3x3 Africa Cup

Table 15:   FIBA 3x3 Africa Cup medalists in men's category

Year	1st	2nd	3rd
2017	Nigeria	Cote d'Ivoire	Madagascar
2018	Cote d'Ivoire	Uganda	Nigeria
2019	Egypt	Dem. Rep. of Congo	Mali

Table 16:   FIBA 3x3 Africa Cup medalists in women's category

Year	1st	2nd	3rd
2017	Mali	Nigeria	Uganda
2018	Mali	Dem. Rep. of Congo	Togo
2019	Egypt	Mali	Uganda

At the FIBA 3x3 Europe Cup 2019, Serbia's men's team and France's women's team each won gold medals.

The Egypt men's and women's teams won gold medals at the FIBA 3x3 Africa Cup 2019.

4   The FIBA 3x3 Asia Cup

Table 17:   FIBA 3x3 Asia Cup medalists in men's category

Year	1st	2nd	3rd
2013	Qatar	Saudi Arabia	Iran
2017	Mongolia	New Zealand	Australia
2018	Australia	Mongolia	Japan
2019	Australia	Mongolia	China

Table 18:   FIBA 3x3 Asia Cup medalists in women's category

Year	1st	2nd	3rd
2013	India	Mongolia	Turkmenistan
2017	Australia	Malaysia	China
2018	New Zealand	China	Australia
2019	Australia	Kazakhstan	Japan

Both the Australia men's and women's teams won gold medals at FIBA 3x3 Asia Cup 2019.

SIDE EVENTS

With the urban culture of 3x3 and the location of tournaments in city centers, organizers frequently put on side events for extra entertainment. Dunk contests, skills contests, or shoot-out competitions all further entertain crowds and viewers at the events. The dunk contests are arguably the most beloved spectacles. This battle of prowess, where dunks are graded by a jury, is usually saved until almost the very end—right before the final.

Chris Staples (USA).

Vadim Poddubchenko (UKR) was the FIBA 3x3 World Cup 2019 Dunk Contest champion.

Jordan Southreland (USA).

3X3 NATIONAL CHAMPIONSHIPS AND EVENTS ORGANIZED BY NATIONAL BASKETBALL FEDERATIONS

The first official 3x3 national championships with integrated FIBA 3x3 rules were organized in 2011 and were held as one- or two-day standalone events. Some nations, such as Slovenia or Romania, even organized their own official three-on-three streetball championships before 2011 and then simply integrated the new FIBA 3x3 rules. Other smaller basketball countries, including Denmark in 2011 and the Netherlands and Uruguay in 2012, and more prominent hoops nations, such as the USA and Germany in 2012, followed suit and started organizing their first official 3x3 national championships. Those events were organized in different age categories for both men and women during the summer and traditional basketball off-season. First, this allowed national basketball federations to stage a 3x3 event outdoors in urban city centers, and second, it allowed traditional basketball players to compete at those events. However, this changed in 2014 when, due to the 3x3 frenzy in their respective countries, some federations started organizing 3x3 leagues that held numerous events which were run for months during the traditional basketball season. Now athletes could play 3x3 throughout the year—indoors during the winter and outdoors during the summer. To further distinguish them from traditional basketball competitions and to enable 3x3 players to turn professional, some national federations (mostly in Asia) went even further and started establishing their own official 3x3 professional leagues, a prime example being China with the CBA 3x3 league and the Philippines with Chooks-to-Go Pilipinas 3x3 league.

Besides organizing 3x3 events, national basketball federations followed the FIBA 3x3 model and created departments within their organizations solely devoted to 3x3. The goals of these departments were:

★ the promotion of 3x3 in their countries

★ the development of regional networks of 3x3 events

★ training players, coaches, referees, and organizers for 3x3 events

★ receiving ranking points in the FIBA 3x3 individual world ranking for the nation's 3x3 players

★ upgrading of the nation's rating in the FIBA 3x3 federation ranking

3X3 EVENTS AND COMPETITIONS BY PRIVATE ORGANIZERS

Just like national federations, established organizers of streetball tournaments and new private promoters worldwide were attracted to 3x3 in 2011 and started staging 3x3 single events, tours, and leagues. These tournaments were at first organized only for recreational purposes, but after 2014, private organizers started organizing professional leagues and single events with higher prizes, attracting better 3x3 players and bigger crowds. In 2012, the NBA formed a global basketball tour called the NBA 3x Tour, which went from continent to continent and city to city, promoting 3x3 basketball. They had support from NBA stars such as James Harden and offered fun side activities for people to take part in. Most important, 3x3 private organizers played a vital role in 3x3 becoming the key motor for the development of basketball worldwide as they helped grow basketball's profile in countries that hadn't traditionally played it. Many private organizers chose to stage a 3x3 event rather than form a traditional basketball league because organizational costs were lower, and it didn't need as much infrastructure.

3X3 BASKETBALL ★

Notable 3x3 Leagues and Tours by Private Organizers Around the World

★ Asia

- The 3x3.EXE Premier is the first professional international 3x3 league. It was created in Japan in 2014. The 2019 men's 3x3 season consisted of multiple conferences, boasting 64 teams playing in four Asian countries. The league consists of both men's and women's competitions.

- The Sina 3x3 Golden League was created in China in 2014. Its fifth season attracted approximately 120,000 players from 30,000 teams representing 185 cities across 30 provinces in China.

- India's 3BL league was created in 2018. Six teams in the women's and 12 teams in men's competition battled in the league's second season. This 3x3 league has been vital in growing the popularity of basketball in India—a country of one billion people addicted to its national sport of cricket. India's finest basketball players and ex-NBA draftees, such as Satnam Singh, have played in this league.

★ USA

- American 3baller, Hoop It Up and other private organizers have been staging 3x3 events and tours and organizing leagues in the United States since 2012. Importantly, the NBA has massively stoked the popularity of 3x3 basketball in the States by organizing the Dew NBA 3x Tour in 2016 and 2017. The Dew NBA 3x Tour staged events across the country with its ambassador, NBA hall of famer Gary Payton. Other NBA players and legends frequently showed up at events to support the new basketball discipline. Consequently, this tour had big impact on 3x3's consideration for the Olympic program in 2017.

★ Europe

- The 3x3 United League Europe is played in Russia and was created in 2018. This is the strongest professional 3x3 league in Europe. Twelve teams from nine countries participated in the 2019 season, and the events did not clash with the FIBA 3x3 Pro Circuit season.

The 3x3.EXE Premier 2019 Final was staged in a lively entertainment district in Tokyo, Japan.

3x3.EXE Premier: the first international professional 3x3 league.

3x3 School Competitions

3x3 has been played by student athletes at elementary school, secondary school, and university levels. The most prominent 3x3 event for student athletes in the USA is the 3x3U National Championship, where the best college basketball players showcase their talents. The championship was first organized in 2018 and is played by players from the best NCAA conferences, such as the Big 10, Big 12, and Big East. The 2019 championship team consisted of Jarrell Brantley, Devontae Cacok, Vasa Pušica, and Justin Wright-Foreman. The team collected more than $100,000 USD in prize money, highlighting the considerable remuneration opportunities for student athletes. Later that year, Brantley and Wright-Foreman were picked up in the 2019 NBA draft, and Cacok won the NBA championship with the Los Angeles Lakers in the 2019/2020 NBA season.

3x3 World Ranking System

There are three types of FIBA 3x3 world rankings: the 3x3 Individual World Ranking, the 3x3 Team World Ranking, and the 3x3 Federation Ranking.

The 3x3 Individual World Ranking

The FIBA 3x3 Individual World Ranking is a ranking of all players registered on play.fiba3x3.com and is based on the nine best player results of the previous 12 months. The number of points earned by a player at an event depends on 1) the event's importance in the competition network (ranking color); 2) the team's results; and 3) the player's individual scoring and key statistical performance (when recorded). It takes time and playing in numerous events to climb the ladder. Dušan Domović Bulut is the all-time points leader in the men's category, while Mamignan Touré of France leads the women's category.

Table 19: All-time FIBA 3x3 individual ranking leaders in
the men's category prior to the 2020 season

Ranking	First Name	Last Name	Country	Total Points
1	Dušan	Domović Bulut	Serbia	4.435.091
2	Marko	Savić	Serbia	3.974.822
3	Dejan	Majstorović	Serbia	3.955.037
4	Simon	Finžgar	Slovenia	2.902.207
5	Mihailo	Vasić	Serbia	2.736.486

The 3x3 Team Ranking

The FIBA 3x3 Team Ranking is calculated by adding up the FIBA 3x3 individual ranking points of the three highest-ranked players from each team. It is used at the start of the season to determine which teams preferentially qualify for the Pro Circuit. It is also used during the season for team seeding at tournaments and at the end of the season to determine the year-end bonus for the top-ranked teams.

The 3x3 Federation Ranking

The FIBA 3x3 Federation Ranking is the ranking of all national federations based on the 3x3 Individual World Ranking points of their top 50 players with a confirmed FIBA 3x3 account in the respective category (combined, men's, women's, U23 men's, U23 women's, U18 men's, U18 women's). It is used for automatic allocations to the Olympic Games and World Cups. It doesn't only reward elite team performances but also the 3x3 activity in the territory of each national federation.

3x3 BASKETBALL ⋆

Table 20: FIBA 3x3 Federation Ranking in combined, men's, and women's
categories, frozen April 1, 2020, due to the Covid-19 pandemic

	Combined	Men's	Women's
1st	Russia	Serbia	France
2nd	USA	USA	China
3rd	France	Russia	Russia
4th	China	Slovenia	Japan
5th	Netherlands	Latvia	Netherlands

CHAPTER 3
THE RULES OF 3X3

3X3'S OFFICIAL RULES COMPARED WITH TRADITIONAL BASKETBALL'S

Before playing or watching 3x3, it is necessary to understand its rules, which are simple and designed to make it fast and exciting. The rules of 3x3 are based on the rules of traditional basketball, but with some modification. Rules relating to dribbling, passing, and shooting have been retained. Unique to 3x3 are rules that determine the court's dimensions, the participants in the game and their duties, time limits, and penalties, among other things. FIBA 3x3 official competitions are played with a specially designed 3x3 ball and on a specially manufactured floor, but at the grassroots level, 3x3 can be played anywhere with traditional basketball equipment and with court markings adapted to the available space. Let's explore the official FIBA 3x3 rules in more detail and see their biggest differences from traditional basketball's.

3x3 BASKETBALL ★

Table 21: Notable similarities and differences in the rules of 3x3 and traditional basketball

Rule	3x3	Traditional Basketball
Baskets	1	2
Basket height	3.05m (10 ft)	3.05m (10 ft)
Hoop diameter	45.72cm (18 inches)	45.72cm (18 inches)
Court size	15 m x 11 m (49.21 ft x 36.09 ft)—the hoop is centered on one of the 15m lines	• FIBA: 15 m x 28 m (49.21 ft x 91.86) • NBA: 15.24 m x 28.65 (50 ft x 94 ft)
Teams	Two teams. Each team shall consist of no more than 4 players. • 3 players on the court + 1 substitute • Teams must start the game with 3 players on the court	Two teams. Each team shall consist of no more than 12 players. • 5 players on the court + 7 substitutes • Teams must start the game with 5 players on the court
Playing time	1 period of 10 min	• FIBA: 4 periods of 10 min • NBA: 4 periods of 12 min
Shot clock	12 sec	24 sec
Winner	• The team with the higher score at the end of regulation time wins. • "Sudden death" rule: The first team to score 21 points or more wins the game if it happens before the end of regular playing time (this is not relevant to overtime).	• The team with the higher score at the end of regulation time wins. • No "sudden death" rule.
Overtime	The first team to score 2 points in overtime wins.	An additional period of 5 minutes is played. As many overtime periods are played as needed until one team wins.

Rule	3x3	Traditional Basketball
Ball	FIBA 3x3: 72 cm (28.5 in) circumference, 624 g (22 oz)—these measurements don't fit a standard ball size category	• NBA and FIBA senior men's competitions: size 7 ball, or 75cm (29.5 in) circumference and 624 g (22 oz) • WNBA and FIBA senior women's competition: size 6 ball, or 72cm (28.5 in) circumference and 567g (20 oz)
Beginning of the game	Coin toss: The team that wins the coin toss determines whether or not to start the game with possession of the ball. If it decides not to take possession of the ball, it is entitled to possession of the ball in any potential overtime.	Jump ball: The referee throws the ball up in the middle of the court, where two players battle for possession in the air.
Scoring rules	• 1 point for a made free throw or made shot from within the two-point arc • 2 points for a made shot from outside the two-point arc	• 1 point for a made free throw • 2 points for a made shot from inside the three-point line • 3 points for a made shot from outside the three-point line
Free-throw line distance from the basket	4.60 m	• FIBA: 4.60 m • NBA: 4.57m (15 ft)
Two-point line / three-point line distance from the basket	6.75m (22.15 ft), and 6.60m (21.65 ft) on the baseline	• FIBA: 6.75m (22.15 ft) and 6.60m (21.65 ft) on the baseline • NBA: 7.24m (23.75 ft) and 6.70m (22 ft) on the baseline
In-game coaching	Not allowed	Allowed

(continued)

(Tab. 21, continued)

Rule	3x3	Traditional Basketball
Time-out	Each team is granted 1. All time-outs last 30 sec.	• FIBA: Each team is granted 2 in the first half, 3 in second half, and 1 per overtime period. Time-outs always last 60 sec. • NBA: Each team is granted 6 and 2 per overtime period. Time-outs last 60 or 100 sec. Each team also has 1 short time-out (20 sec) per half. There are additional regulations.
Referees	1 or 2 per game in senior competitions	2 or 3 per game in senior competitions
How the ball is played following any dead-ball situation	Possession starts with a check-ball at the top of the two-point arc. The ball is exchanged between the defensive and offensive player.	Possession starts with an inbound pass from outside the court.
How the ball is played following each successful field goal or last free throw (except those followed by ball possession)	• A player from a non-scoring team shall resume the game by dribbling or passing the ball from inside the court directly underneath the basket to a place on the court behind the two-point arc. A player must first clear the ball behind the two-point arc before a scoring attempt. • A player from the scoring team is not allowed to play for the ball in the no-charge semicircle area underneath the basket.	• A player from a non-scoring team shall inbound the ball from the endline (outside the court).

Rule	3x3	Traditional Basketball
How the ball is played following a steal and each unsuccessful field goal or last free throw (except those followed by ball possession)	• An offensive player who rebounds the ball may continue to attempt to score without returning the ball behind the two-point arc. • A defensive player who rebounds or steals the ball inside the two-point arc must first clear the ball behind the two-point arc before making a score attempt. • A defensive player who rebounds or steals the ball outside the two-point arc does not need to clear the ball behind the two-point arc before making a score attempt.	• An offensive player who rebounds the ball may continue to attempt to score. • A defensive player who rebounds or steals the ball may attempt to score immediately on the opposing basket.
Clearance	A player is considered to be behind the two-point arc when neither feet are inside or on the arc line.	There is no need to clear the ball after a change of possession.

(continued)

(Tab. 21, continued)

Rule	3x3	Traditional Basketball
Jump balls and alternating possession	In the event of a held ball/jump ball, the game shall be resumed with a check-ball for the last defensive team. The shot clock shall be reset to 12 seconds.	• FIBA: A jump ball starts the game. The team that loses the initial jump ball gets the next possession. Possession alternates between teams thereafter in held ball/jump ball situations. • NBA: A jump ball starts the game. The team that loses the initial jump ball gets possession to start 2nd and 4th quarters. The team that wins the initial jump ball gets possession to start 3rd quarter. All held ball/jump ball situations are resolved by a jump ball.
Personal foul bonus	No personal foul bonus	• FIBA: 5 fouls • NBA: 6 fouls
Team foul bonus	6 fouls	4 fouls in a quarter
Number of free throws for 5th and 6th team fouls (in 1 quarter for traditional basketball)	0—possession starts with a check-ball	2
Number of free throws for 7th, 8th, and 9th team foul (in 1 quarter for traditional basketball)	2	2

Rule	3x3	Traditional Basketball
Number of free throws for tenth and subsequent team fouls (in 1 quarter for traditional basketball)	2 + possession of the ball	2
Number of free throw(s) after a foul in the act of shooting when a shot is missed	• 1 for a 1-point shot attempt until the 7th team foul • 2 for a shot outside the two-point arc • 2 in the case of 7th, 8th and 9th team fouls • 2 + possession in the case of the 10th and every subsequent team foul	• 2 in the case of a foul inside the 3-point arc • 3 in the case of a foul outside the 3-point arc
Number of free throw(s) awarded after a foul in the act of shooting and when a shot is made	• 1 until the 7th team foul • 2 in the case of the 7th, 8th and 9th team fouls • 2 + possession in the case of the 10th and every subsequent team foul	1
Technical foul by an offensive player	The fouled team is awarded 1 free throw. Following the free throw, the ball remains in the possession of the offensive team before the foul was called. Time on shot clock remains the same as before the foul.	The fouled team is awarded 1 free throw. Following the free throw, the ball remains in the possession of the offensive team before the foul was called. Time on shot clock remains the same as before the foul.
Technical foul by a defensive player	The fouled team is awarded 1 free throw. The team that was last in possession of the ball keeps possession.	The fouled team is awarded 1 free throw. The team that was last in possession of the ball keeps possession.

(continued)

3x3 BASKETBALL ★

(Tab. 21, continued)

Rule	3x3	Traditional Basketball
Unsportsmanlike foul	The fouled team is awarded 2 free throws, and 2 fouls are added for the record.	The fouled team is awarded 2 free throws and possession of the ball.
Disqualifying fouls	A player committing 2 unsportsmanlike fouls will be disqualified from the game by the referees and from the event by the organizer. All disqualifying fouls shall be penalized with 2 free throws.	A player committing 2 unsportsmanlike fouls will be disqualified.
Instant replay system (challenge)	Teams at top-level FIBA 3x3 events are allowed one challenge per game. Referees review the decision through video analysis, and if the challenge is won, the team gets possession and retains its allocation of one challenge. If the team loses a challenge, then the team is left with no more challenges for the rest of the game.	Not available.
Semicircle	A defensive player must not step inside the semicircle after a made basket. The team will be penalized first with a warning, while every subsequent obstruction inside the semicircle is counted as a technical foul. Moreover, the semicircle is used as a no-offensive-charge space.	Used as a no-offensive-charge space.

Rule	3x3	Traditional Basketball
Stalling rule	Stalling, or failing to play actively, is a violation. An offensive player, after the ball has been cleared, shall not hold the ball and/or dribble inside the arc with his or her back or side to the basket for more than 5 consecutive seconds.	This rule does not exist.
Substitutions	Players may be substituted in the event of a referee's interruption without the intervention of a referee. A substitute may enter the game after a teammate steps off the court and makes physical contact behind the back line of the court.	The substitute who is to enter the game must remain off the court until the referee allows and signals for the substitution to go ahead.

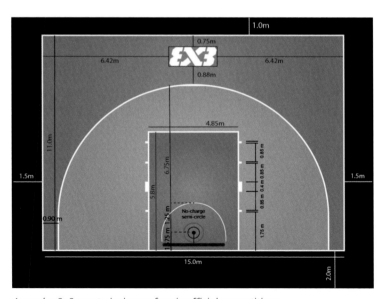

A regular 3x3 court playing surface in official competitions.

THE HISTORY AND EVOLUTION OF 3X3 RULES

The first official rules of the "3on3 basketball game" (as the sport was still referred to at this time) were presented in 2007 by FIBA and used later that year at the Asian Indoor Games in Macau, where 3on3 basketball was played as a demonstration sport. In contrast to the rules used now, the game started with a jump ball at the free-throw line, consisted of two halves of eight minutes each, had an offensive shot clock set to 16 seconds, and had the same scoring rules as in traditional basketball. Sweeping changes to the rules were presented by FIBA 3x3 in 2010 and FIBA 3x3 has continued to tweak them over the years. The rules of 3x3 have been changing and adapting as FIBA 3x3 bids to quicken the game and make it a fast and furious spectacle.

Even one rule change can make a huge difference to a sport. Notably, the NBA's adding the 24-second shot clock in 1954 quickly changed the game's pace and increased scoring by putting an end to stalling tactics. Scoring went up from 79.5 points per game in the 1953–1954 season to 93.1 points per game in the 1954–1955 season.

There have been many notable 3x3 rule changes, but some basic rules have stayed the same since its official inception. These include all the rules regarding dribbling violations, clearing the ball behind the arc after receiving a basket, playing on one basket, and teams being made up of three starting players and one substitute, among others.

Three-on-Three Streetball Rules

Long before 3x3 became a formal basketball discipline, people loved to play three-on-three streetball on one basket ("twenty-one") on outdoor courts for recreation. The 3x3's predecessor didn't just heavily influence 3x3 basketball culture, but it also set basis for the current official rules of 3x3. Twenty-one doesn't have official rules, but its unofficial rules are nearly the same all over the world. The most basic twenty-one rules are nearly identical to current 3x3 rules: In both, a game is played on one basket with three players per team, and the first team to score 21 points wins the game. Moreover, both have the same scoring and dribbling rules and no personal foul limit. After a defensive team has rebounded the ball inside the two-point arc, teams have to first clear the ball outside the two-point arc before they can score. However, there are significant rule differences that sets these two games apart. Compared to 3x3 in its current form, twenty-one isn't as fast paced because it lacks an offensive shot clock, a team foul bonus, and has more frequent dead ball situations. Different from 3x3, where after each basket teams change possession and the play immediately continues, an offensive team in twenty-one stays on offense after each scored basket and starts a new play with the check ball at the top of the two-point arc which strongly influences the pace of the game. Furthermore, in pick-up 21, a two-point win differential is necessary; there are no referees; and players must call fouls. The latter is from where the game's and 3x3's innate aggressiveness has evolved. It is evident that 3x3 rules proceed from both official basketball rules and unofficial 3-on-3 streetball rules. While some rules have been retained, others have been heavily modified.

Notable 3x3 Rule Changes Over the Years

2010–2013

In 2010, FIBA 3x3 modified their first rules without compromising the free spirit of street basketball. However, 3x3 rules back then were still much different from the current version. For instance, at the first official 3x3 international event, 3x3 was played on a traditional basketball half-court, with both teams shooting on one hoop over two five-minute periods. It was fast-paced, with a 10-second shot clock for an attacking side and no time-outs, while teams could win before the end of regulation by being the first to 33 points. At that time, in-game coaching was allowed, but not dunking unless pressure-released rings were used. Scoring was three points for a made shot from behind the arc, two for one inside the arc, and one point for a made free throw. These rules, which were similar to traditional basketball, were later modified, as FIBA wanted its new discipline to have more of its own identity.

3x3 really started to take shape and look like the game of today at the 2011 U18 3x3 World Cup, where the shot clock was set to 12 seconds and 21 points were needed in order for a team to win the game in regulation time. The scoring system changed to what we have grown to love: two points from beyond the arc and one point from inside. The change of scoring meant the two-pointer was worth twice as much as a shot inside the arc, incentivizing the long-range bombs that are such a breathtaking part of basketball.

2013–2015

In 2013, FIBA 3x3 modified rules and increased the point value for a dunk to two points—the same amount awarded for a shot from behind the arc. After carefully watching how the rules impacted the game during the year, FIBA returned to awarding a single point for a dunk.

In 2014, FIBA 3x3 made important rule changes in order to further speed up the game. They implemented a team foul bonus at six team fouls, awarding the fouled team two free throws when the threshold is reached. After the 10th team foul, the opposing team is awarded two free throws and possession of the ball. This rule was deemed necessary to maintain the game's speedy pace and to punish overtly physical defense. Personal foul rules that expelled players from the game after five fouls were scrapped. Importantly, whenever the defensive team gained the ball inside the two-point arc, even through a steal, they had to clear the ball behind the arc.

In 2015, the penalty for a technical foul was downgraded from two free throws and possession to one free throw and possession.

2016–2020

Between 2016 and 2020, FIBA 3x3 continued making significant rule changes to further differentiate itself from traditional basketball.

In 2016, FIBA 3x3 expended the offensive rule called stalling, where failing to play actively is a violation. From this point on, dribbling inside the arc with the back turned to the basket for more than five consecutive seconds was a violation of the rules. This encouraged more face-to-face play and ensured better aesthetics. In an important move—one that clearly differentiated 3x3 from traditional basketball—coaches were not allowed in the playing area, and teams were penalized with a technical foul for in-game coaching. FIBA 3x3 also adapted the U12 categories to create a more suitable environment for that age group and to make the game more attractive to kids.

In 2017, FIBA 3x3 released its rule interpretations and clarified its decision-making. Subsequently, challenges were implemented, underlining the benefits of the instant replay system, which trials in 2016 showed clearly helped officials with their decision-making.

In 2018, one of the primary goals of referees was to increase protection for shooters and skillful players while cracking down on situations like pushing, grabbing, and screening—especially in pick and roll situations—and movement without the ball.

Vlad Ghizdareanu, FIBA 3x3 referee:

"Every year, we focused on a specific rule (or more) to clean up the game and encourage skillful players, and on August 29, 2019, the "Official 3x3 Basketball Rules" manual was released, and we no longer made reference to the five-on-five game."[28]

3X3 BASKETBALL ★

Table 22: Evolution of the official 3x3 rules

Rule	2007	2010	After 2011
Court size	Half of a traditional FIBA basketball court (15 m x 14 m)	Half of a traditional FIBA basketball court (15 m x 14 m)	15m x 11m (2012)
Beginning of the game	Jump ball at the free-throw line.	Team A begins the game with a throw-in opposite the scorer's table; team B is entitled to the ball in the next jump ball situation in accordance with alternating possession.	The team that wins a coin toss can choose possession of the ball at the start of the game or in overtime. Teams start the game with a check-ball at the top in the middle of the two-point arc. (2011)
Regular time	2 periods of 8 min	2 periods of 5 min	1 period of 10 min (2011)
Sudden death rule	21 points	33 points	21 points (2011)
Overtime	As many extra periods of 2 min as are necessary to break the tie	As many extra periods of 2 min as are necessary to break the tie	First team to score 2 points wins the game (2011)
Value of a made shot beyond the arc	3 points	3 points	2 points (2011)
Value of a made shot inside the arc	2 points	2 points	1 point (2011)
Offensive shot clock	16 sec	10 sec	12 sec (2011)
Time-outs per game	2	0	1 (2011)
In-game coaching	Allowed	Allowed	Not allowed (2016)

Rule	2007	2010	After 2011
How the ball is played following each successful field goal or last free throw	A player from the non-scoring team resumes the game by passing the ball to a teammate in any place on the court behind the three-point line.	A player from a non-scoring team resumes the game from directly underneath the basket either by passing the ball to a teammate anywhere on the court (but if not behind the three-point arc, the receiver has to dribble or pass the ball behind the three-point arc) or by dribbling the ball to a place behind the three-point arc.	A player from the non-scoring team resumes the game from directly underneath the basket either by passing the ball to a teammate anywhere on the court (but if not behind the three-point arc, the receiver has to dribble or pass the ball behind the three-point arc) or by dribbling the ball to a place behind the three-point arc.
Player from scoring team must be positioned outside semicircle after a made basket	No	Yes	Yes
Once the ball is cleared...	A minimum of two players have to touch the ball before a scoring attempt.	At least one additional pass has to be made to a teammate before a scoring attempt.	A player can immediately attempt to score. (2011)
Throw-ins from out of bounds	Yes	Yes	No (2011)

(continued)

3X3 BASKETBALL ★

(Tab. 22, continued)

Rule	2007	2010	After 2011
Throw-ins following fouls (without free throws), violations, or out-of-bounds situations	Throw-ins are from out of bounds, level with the top of the three-point arc opposite the scorer's table. The place is marked by a 5 cm line.	Throw-ins are from out of bounds, level with the top of the three-point arc, opposite the scorer's table. The place is marked by a 5 cm line.	No throw-ins. An offensive play starts inside the court with a check-ball (exchanging the ball between an offensive and defensive player at the top of the two-point arc). (2011)
Personal foul limit	4	5	No personal foul limit (2014)
Team foul bonus	4 in a half—2 free throws awarded to fouled team after every subsequent team foul	4 in a half—2 free throws awarded to fouled team after every subsequent team foul	6 in the game—2 free throws awarded to fouled team after every subsequent team foul, plus possession starting with the 10th (2014)
Stalling rule	None	None	Implemented (2011)
Dunking	Not permitted unless pressure-released rings are in use	Not permitted unless pressure-released rings are in use	Allowed in all circumstances (2011)
Penalty for technical foul	2 free throws and possession	2 free throws and possession	• 1 free throw and possession (2015) • 1 free throw (2019)
Penalty for unsportsmanlike foul	2 free throws and possession	2 free throws and possession	2 free throws (2019)

Rule	2007	2010	After 2011
Adapted rules for younger categories (U12)	None	None	Implemented to create a proper environment for that age and make it more attractive for kids (2016)
Instant replay system (challenges)	None	None	1 challenge per team (2017)

CHAPTER 4
3X3 THEORY AND GAME STRUCTURE

3X3 GAME STRUCTURE

This chapter lays out the game structure of 3x3 theoretically as well as introducing 3x3 terminology. Like traditional basketball, 3x3 is a multi-structured and complex team game.[29] Games are played in regular time for 10 minutes at most or until any team scores 21 points or more. In overtime, when the game is tied after regular time has expired, the game is played until one of the teams scores 2 points. There is one big difference between regular time and overtime: in both, the shot clock runs, but in regular time a game clock is turned on while in overtime there is no game clock. It is important to know that for the team and players, a 3x3 game always consists of active phases when teams are playing—are allowed to play (e.g., live ball) and passive phases when teams are not playing—are not allowed to play (e.g., dead ball). In the active phases, players experience predominantly anaerobic exercise, while in passive phases they experience predominantly aerobic exercise. An active phase consists of many subphases. The number of subphases in the active phase can vary considerably based on a team's pace and ability to hit 21 points.

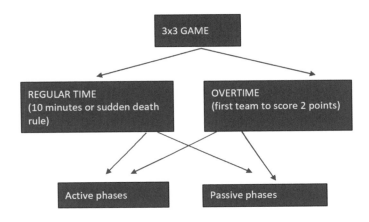

Active Subphases

Active game phases in both 3x3 and traditional basketball have offensive, defensive, and intermediate phases. In both disciplines, the offensive team switches to defense when they lose possession of the ball, and the defensive team switches to offense when they gain possession of the ball. However, there are some differences in the rules that make 3x3's offensive and defensive phases completely unique. In traditional basketball, a team can start an offensive play with inbound pass from either the baseline or the sideline, but in 3x3, every play must start inside the court. So instead, 3x3's offensive and defensive phases consist of transition and check-ball phases that are determined by where and how a team has gained possession.

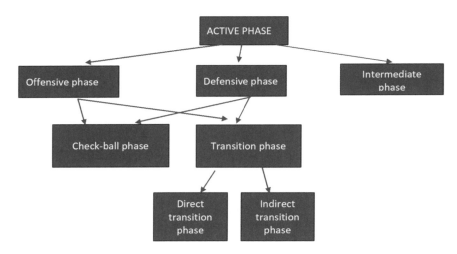

Definitions

★ An **offensive phase** consists of one or more subphases. In 3x3, the offensive phase of one team lasts from the moment a team gains possession of the live ball until 1) a shot is made and the ball goes through the hoop; 2) the ball bounces off the hoop after a missed shot; 3) the referee stops play due to a foul, turnover, or any other another event (e.g., injury); or 4) the opposing team acquires possession of the ball (e.g., a steal). The offense's goals are to maintain possession of the ball, keep the ball moving, and score 21 points before the other team, or at least have scored more points than the opponent at the end of regulation time.

★ A **defensive phase** is directly opposite to an offensive phase and consists of one or more subphases. A team is on defense from the moment the offensive team gains possession of the ball until the offensive team loses possession through a made field goal or last free throw (not followed by possession), a turnover, or a missed field goal or last free throw (not followed by possession) that is rebounded by the defensive team. A defensive team's goal is to minimize their opponent's possessions and stop them from scoring.

★ An **intermediate phase** is located between the offensive and defensive phases. This is the period in which the ball is not in the possession of either team. It lasts from the moment the ball bounces off the hoop after a missed shot or falls through the hoop after the completed shot to the moment a player of one of the teams acquires possession of the live ball (through a rebound or by picking up the ball after a made basket), or until the referee's whistle calling a foul or other play stoppage.

★ A **check-ball phase** is part of the offensive and defensive phase. It starts at the moment a check ball in the middle top of the two-point arc is complete (i.e., the ball is exchanged between the defensive and the offensive players). In 3x3, possession of the ball given to either team following any dead-ball situation starts with a check ball. At that point, the dead ball becomes live. Compared to the transition phase, the check-ball phase happens less frequently during a 3x3 game.

★ A **transition phase** is part of the offensive and defensive phase. It starts the moment possession of the ball changes in the active phase, whether through a defensive rebound, a steal, or by picking up the ball after opponent's made basket that is not followed by possession. While traditional basketball only has a vertical transition, 3x3's are horizontal, diagonal, or vertical. A transition phase is further divided depending on where and how a defensive team acquires possession of the ball.

★ A **direct transition phase** is a part of the transition phase and starts when possession changes in the active phase in such a way that a defensive player gains possession of the ball outside the two-point arc. A team, after gaining a possession, is allowed to immediately shoot on the basket.

★ An **indirect transition phase** is a part of the transition phase and starts when possession changes in the active phase in such a way that a defensive player gains possession of the ball inside the two-point arc. A team, after gaining a possession, needs to first clear the ball with a dribble or a pass outside the two-point arc before it is allowed to shoot on the basket.

Transition Phase vs. Check-ball Phase

3x3 teams are constantly switching from defense to offense and vice versa due to the short shot clock. When analyzing the structure of the offense, it is important to know that a transition offense happens two to three times more often than a check-ball offense but this depends mostly on the number of dead-ball situations and differs from one game to the next, underlining the importance of teams devoting more time in training to developing an efficient transition offense.

Table 23: Differences between a transition offense and a check-ball offense

	Transition Offense	Check-ball Offense
Start of the offensive play	After a defensive rebound, steal, or gained possession after a completed basket	After a check-ball in the top middle of the two-point arc is complete
Occurrence	During an active phase	Directly after the passive phase (so players have more time to prepare for the offensive play)
Starting player position	Anywhere on the court	In the top middle of the two-point arc
Teammate positions	Their prior positions on defense	Based on team organization and preference
When a scoring attempt can be made	• Indirect: after a player clears the ball with a pass or a dribble outside the two-point arc • Direct: immediately	Once the check-ball is complete
Time to complete the offensive play from the moment a team can make a scoring attempt	Less than 12 secs if possession is acquired inside the two-point arc; 12 secs if possession is acquired outside the two-point arc	12 secs
Frequency	Occurs more often	Occurs less often
Playing style	More improvisational	More organized
Tactics	More complex and harder to predict	Less complex and easier to predict

Table 24: Differences between transition defense and check-ball defense

	Transition Defense	Check-ball Defense
Start of the defensive play	After an opponent's defensive rebound, steal, or gained possession after a made basket	After a check-ball in the top middle of the two-point arc is complete
Occurrence	During an active phase	Directly after a passive phase
Guarding offensive players at the start of an offensive play	Defensive players do not have time to arrange as they wish. Normally they are forced to guard the closest opponent.	Defensive players can arrange and select whom they wish to guard.
Defensive organization	Less organized. It is hard to properly organize and establish on defense due to rapid transition.	Better organized
Characterization	Situational decision-making where players mostly "read and react"	Predetermined tactics, which help against schematic and organized plays
Frequency	Happens more frequently.	Happens less frequently.

Every play starts inside the court. After a check-ball is complete, the ball is live.

3x3 Defense vs. Traditional Basketball Defense

There are differences between a 3x3 defense and a traditional basketball defense, but the fundamental principles are the same. The biggest difference—and a new thing for players transitioning from basketball to 3x3—is in how to efficiently guard players before the ball is cleared in the transition phase. This will be explained later in the book. These are the other fundamental differences between defense in 3x3 and traditional basketball:

★ 3x3 is a high-contact, physical game. Referees allow more contact by defenders, who can use this to help stop drives to the basket and obstruct opponents' movement. Defensive players can use more hand-checking, pushing, and holding compared to traditional basketball. Notably, in the NBA, hand-checking of perimeter players was made illegal in the mid-2000s in an effort to increase scoring.

★ 3x3 defense is more focused on defenders being able to guard one-on-one, containing the ball and stopping two-point shots.

★ 3x3 defensive teams often allow layups in preference to two-point shots.

★ 3x3 defensive players guarding off-ball players provide less purposeful help coverage due to greater space. They can't pack the paint when they are primarily guarding an offensive player on a two-point arc, and their help drop is not as deep as in basketball.

★ Switching is more common in 3x3, while rejecting screens and double-teaming is very rare.

★ 3x3 defenders spend more of their time in low stance, which allows them quick lateral movements and reactions to curb opponents. This is stressful on the body and contrasts with traditional basketball, where defenders tend to run back to their basket before positioning in low stance.

★ Defensive weaknesses are usually exposed in 3x3 due to more open space and the lack of players, meaning there isn't anywhere to hide.

3x3 Transition Defense vs. Traditional Basketball Transition Defense

In traditional basketball, players have time to run back, listen to their coach, take a breather, and organize after each made basket. However in 3x3, the play after a made basket is immediately live, and the game is played only on one hoop, so players in transition need to be focused every second and stick close to opponents. These are the fundamental differences between a 3x3 transition defense and traditional basketball transition defense:

★ 3x3 defensive players have less time to establish and organize.

★ 3x3 transitions create more mismatches because teams are often forced to switch in order to prevent a quick and open shot.

⋆ There is little or no time to celebrate made baskets, dispute bad calls, or argue with teammates, since the game moves very quickly. Composure and concentration are keys to a successful 3x3 transition defense.

⋆ 3x3 defensive players are forced into matchups based on the prior play. Most commonly, because of the game's fast nature and short shot clock, players guard the closest opponent. Communication is essential for a team to execute a transition defense properly.

Make defensive communication a habit. It can be utterly damaging if a team fails to communicate in transition from offense to defense.

CHAPTER 5
THE UNIQUENESS OF 3X3

THE CHARACTER OF 3X3

According to FIBA, 3x3 stands for nonstop basketball, excitement, and fun. 3x3 was inspired by and is strongly connected to traditional basketball and streetball, but that connection was largely severed when 3x3's official rules were instituted and the game formed its own identity.

Definition

3x3 is a contact team game played on one basket by two teams of three players each. Teams try to score a basket by shooting a ball through a hoop elevated 3.05 meters (10 feet) above the ground. A team wins if it scores 21 points first or has scored more points by the end of the regulated time period of 10 minutes.

Accessibility, Approachability, and Non-Commitment

The organizational form and rules of 3x3 contribute to its accessible, approachable, and non-committal character. The accessibility of 3x3 is an important element of the game that is reflected in various ways. 3x3 can be played indoors and outdoors all year round and is simple and flexible enough to be enjoyed by players of all levels and genders in a professional, developmental, or recreational setting. To play a 3x3 game, six players only need a basketball court or a playground with one basket and a ball. There might not always be sufficient numbers to play a traditional basketball game, but its easier to get just enough players for 3x3. In contrast to the professional level, mostly organized by FIBA 3x3, grassroots competitions are organized by either national federations or private promoters and represent the majority of events. Entry requirements for those grassroots events are set low so that they are easily accessible through an online platform where prior playing experience is not necessary. Almost all teams that apply are allowed to compete, and this leads to large numbers of teams in grassroots tournaments as organizers try to ensure all of them to take part and have fun. The simple nature of getting involved in 3x3 is crucial to its success and so too is non-commitment where players in 3x3 are not tied to a club or team and can experiment playing with whomever they wish at grassroots events. Furthermore, FIBA 3x3's ambitious motto of "from the streets to the world stage" is an important brand because it illustrates an enticing pathway for all players. FIBA 3x3's system means teams have to start from the bottom but can work their way up to the elite level. FIBA also has a strong desire for 3x3 to spread to all parts of the world and to ensure equal opportunity—a key focus of 3x3—FIBA 3x3 makes it feasible for every nation to play at World Cups and other tournaments.

Last but not least, children can easily be a part of 3x3 as the application process is arranged more informally than in traditional basketball, where a child must first join a club, participate in training, and pay monthly or yearly fees before playing in a league.

To play 3x3 with a team, a person can register just a day or two ahead of a tournament and doesn't have to be a member of a federation or league. This non-committal character of 3x3 represents a great way for youth to be introduced to the game of basketball. 3x3 is also easily approachable by fans through free online streaming platforms and with free entries at events in most city centers.

Events can be staged outdoors, like the WT in Lausanne, Switzerland.

Justice Winslow, NBA player:

"I think more people are getting into it because it's a fun, easy sport. It's not like other sports where you need all this equipment."[30]

Dennis Scott, former NBA star:

"I think this brand of basketball has a chance to take over the world....Now, kids can say, you know what, I didn't make my basketball high school team, but I think I can make this 3x3 team, or create my own team and be competitive."[31]

Events can be staged indoors, like the WT in Manila, Philippines.

Formalization and Institutionalization

3x3 has evolved from its streetball origins, gained strict rules, established federations and a structured playing platform. Now FIBA 3x3 governs the game. While the links between traditional basketball and 3x3 are obvious, FIBA was keen to establish 3x3 on its own feet and not rely on traditional basketball's heft. Even though 3x3 has become a formalized discipline, FIBA has ensured that entry requirements are set very low to grow the game in its infancy. FIBA is working hard to distinguish 3x3 from traditional basketball both on and off the court. On court, a prime example is 3x3's unique ball. While in traditional basketball, size and weight of the ball differ for men and women, in 3x3, both categories use the same ball. In 3x3, the size of the ball compared to one used in male basketball competition is smaller to assist players in faster and better ball-handling. However, the ball has the same weight to maintain performances in outdoor conditions. Off-court, the formalization of 3x3 is also represented in its branding (such as its logo), commercial relationships, and administrative independence. The logo was created in 2010 and is at the core of 3x3's identity. Composed of two face-to-face numeral 3s with an x in between, it represents two teams of three players facing off against each other. The snazzy logo is also reminiscent of the infinity symbol, conveying a sense of limitless fun, competition, and excitement.

Globalization

3x3 has been fine-tuning at the international and domestic level since its foundation. The FIBA 3x3 World Cup and World Tour has taken 3x3 all over the map from Los Angeles to several off-beat destinations—like Jeddah in Saudi Arabia—to truly fulfill FIBA's mission in spreading the game to all corners of the globe. 3x3 has also quickly become part of the biggest international sporting events. It featured for the first time in the European Games in 2015, South American and Asian Games in 2018, and Pan American, Pacific, and African Games in 2019. Globalization has helped professional 3x3 in large part through the accessibility of play.fiba3x3.com, which has created a thriving online community and enabled easy access to events worldwide. Visibility is always important for a growing sport, and FIBA has recognized this by broadcasting top 3x3 events for free on YouTube. Other sports networks also now frequently broadcast 3x3 basketball events.

Community

FIBA 3x3 has worked hard at building a community around this discipline, especially at the beginning when most teams didn't have a structure organized by national federations. Once the community was established, socializing during events was common, and this helped younger athletes to develop not only physically but also socially. 3x3 grassroots events involve numerous teams and sometime multiple categories on the same day, where competitors can interact, and this creates a unique atmosphere. It's not just about wins and losses; the essence of 3x3 fuses competitiveness with entertainment and social interaction. Moreover, unlike in traditional basketball, players aren't tied to specific teams at grassroot events during a season, so they can mingle more freely with others without appearing to be disloyal. 3x3 has also importantly established itself as fan friendly, with spectators feeling a level of ownership of the game that is uncommon among other sports.

Location

Most of the 3x3 events are organized outdoors in city center, high-traffic locations, and there is an effort to preserve this characteristic of the game. FIBA 3x3 events bring the sound system, street dance, side shows, and some of the most spectacular dunk contests to historical or scenic locations right in the heart of the city. Thus, events are eye-catching not just for the spectacular on-court action, but also for the stunning backdrop. The events appeal to a young urban audience which guarantees to get hearts pounding—on the court and in the crowd. The atmosphere of an outdoor event in a city center makes for a unique experience, quite different from that of traditional basketball. However, outdoor events are not always practical because of poor weather conditions like wind, rain, and cold, so events can also be organized indoors—most often in shopping malls.

Basically, 3x3 organizers can temporarily and easily structure the court in different locations due to 3x3's simple equipment. This gives another opportunity to entice spectators to watch basketball whether in person in the city center or on the broadcast.

Patrick Baumann, former FIBA secretary general:

"For us, location is key. We want people who are passing by to stop and say, 'This is cool.'"[32]

FIBA 3x3 World Cup 2019 was staged in Amsterdam, Netherlands.

World Tour staged in Chengdu, China.

World Tour staged in Jeddah, Saudi Arabia.

World Tour staged in Debrecen, Hungary.

FUNDAMENTAL IN-GAME DIFFERENCES BETWEEN 3X3 AND BASKETBALL

Current 3x3 events are mostly played by former or current traditional basketball players, as they can frequently transition from one game to another during the year. However, transitioning from traditional basketball to 3x3 can be difficult due to rule changes and the differing types of physical exercise. This creates a learning curve and leads to a difference in how athletes prepare for competition. This section presents some of the fundamental in-game differences from basketball. Other, more detailed differences will be presented in later chapters.

Type of Physical Exercise

3x3 is predominantly anaerobic exercise. It's significantly more anaerobic than traditional basketball. Increased high-intensity accelerations and decelerations from change of direction movements contribute to this difference. On the other hand, the traditional basketball games last longer, and the aerobic endurance is more prevalent than in 3x3.

Although 3x3 is predominantly anaerobic, the development of aerobic capacity is important as it helps players to quickly recover between efforts or during short substitution periods. With better endurance, the performance in the next on-court period can be maintained.[33]

Intensity

3x3 is extremely intense and has been aptly dubbed a "10-minute sprint." Accelerations and short sprints are performed at maximum or sub-maximum intensity. These are interspersed with brief recovery periods. Research has found that 3x3 is two times more intense than traditional basketball. The relative intensity of 3x3 World Tour professional men's players (6.7 ± 1.5) doubles that of professional basketballers from the NBA's development league (3.10 ± 0.9) when player loads are evaluated relative to game time. Player load is a volume measure of player's activity level and gives us an estimate of physical demand.[33] Surprisingly, although there is less total distance covered and games are shorter compared to traditional basketball, the play style of 3x3 drives a stronger physiological response. Normally one might think that success is related to work rate (player load), but this is not the case in the FIBA 3x3 official competitions as there are weak relationships between player load and finishing higher in a tournament or the average number of points scored. The outcomes in 3x3 are more likely defined by skills and other factors.[33]

Contact and Physicality

More contact is allowed in 3x3 than in traditional basketball. The higher levels of contact, collisions, and impacts are an aspect of the game preserved from streetball. 3x3 referees are thus more lenient than in traditional basketball while still protecting the players. There are two referees per game at official FIBA 3x3 events, and they are sometimes reluctant to blow the whistle because it would affect the game's pace. Nevertheless, FIBA 3x3 has found a good balance between nonstop action and player safety. It is obvious that 3x3 players embrace the physical side of the game marked by grabbing, leaning and pushing, which has become one of its appeals. In order to cope with this physical contact, strength, stabilization and power training are extremely important.[3]

Athletes have to be ready for a tough physical battle.

Movement

3x3 requires more fast and sharp changes of direction compared to traditional basketball, with lower body strength being necessary to high levels of competition. Linear, lateral, and rotational movements are a part of both games. Besides quick direction changes, 3x3 player movements include many high-speed accelerations, decelerations, and jumps within a confined playing area.[33–34] Surprisingly, the volume of high-speed accelerations and decelerations are similar between males and females, which appears to be a unique aspect of 3x3 and demonstrates that high-speed movement is not gender-specific. Agility, speed, and repeat sprint training will help 3x3 players improve speed, foot quickness, coordination, and, most important, the ability to change direction with minimal deceleration. [33]

Increased Relative Player Area Coverage

3x3 demands greater movement because players have to cover a greater area (27 square meters) compared to traditional basketball players (21 square meters over a half-court).[34] Because 3x3 is more open and spread out, helping defend in the low post or double-teaming is more difficult which encourages players to take advantage of mismatches.

Emphasis on One-on-One Play

Fewer players and more open space in 3x3 compared to traditional basketball magnifies the importance of each individual player's skills. In this cutting-edge sport, which is fierce and ultra-competitive, every skill of the game is exposed. If a player can't shoot, the defense lays off him. If a player can't defend, offense will take him one-on-one. Even though players choose one-on-one isolation plays frequently in 3x3 due to more open space, teams should not be too reliant on isolation, because that strategy is easy for elite teams to curtail. Instead, they should be aim for ball movement and getting more players involved in the play because it is harder to guard teams using "two-man" or team plays. Unlike in traditional basketball, all players can make effective use of one-on-one post play, as there is less help, and anyone can get on the low block—an area in basketball that is usually reserved for bigger and stronger players.

Lightning Transition and Dynamicity

3x3 is a fast-paced and dynamic basketball discipline, requiring technical, tactical, and athletic abilities. Players are continually upping the pace, which, along with the 12-second shot clock and live play after made baskets, leaves very little time for breaks. As soon as 3x3 players score, they must quickly turn around and get set. Because in traditional basketball a play after a made basket starts with an inbound pass from outside the court, it usually has slower tempo, and players can catch their breath during the more frequent dead-ball situations or when running back and organizing on defense. The immediate play in 3x3's transition phase tests players' endurance and forces them to spend more time on defense in a low defensive stance compared to traditional basketball.

Tactics

Generally, traditional basketball teams tend to use more schematic and organized plays, whereas 3x3 is more spontaneous and instinctive because of shorter shot clock. Players have to read and react based on intuition. Because of more unstructured player movement in 3x3, team's offensive tactics and player's offensive patterns are harder to predict.

Unpredictability and Level Playing Field

When teams have five players that are extremely talented, they can dominate the game in a 40- or 48-minute period, but when there are only three players and a 10-minute period, the playing field is little more leveled. Generally, 3x3 is more unpredictable than traditional basketball because the game can end before the clock runs down if one team reaches or passes 21 points, whereas in traditional basketball regular time is always fixed and there's no sudden death rule. A famous example of 3x3's unpredictability is the unforgettable 2017 World Tour Final, when hot favorite Novi Sad appeared destined for the title, leading by four points in the final match over Zemun with just over one minute left in regulation. Zemun prevailed in one of the most dramatic final minutes of a game ever to defeat Novi Sad and prove that anything is possible in 3x3.

CHAPTER 6
PROFESSIONAL 3X3 TEAMS AND PLAYERS

PROFESSIONALISM

The professionalization of sport not only comprises the player switch from amateur status to a paid professional; or the emergence and development of professional clubs or teams; but also, the delivery of a platform for growing professionalism within the sport. So, to truly be deemed professional, 3x3 needed an annual elite competition, and this was instituted in 2012 when FIBA 3x3 started its Pro Circuit with its pinnacle male competition, the 3x3 World Tour. There were only a few professional teams worldwide at the start, but that number quickly increased with the carrot of prize money to propel 3x3's growth. The sports professionalization by which sport organizations convert from a volunteer-driven to business-like phenomenon generally stems from the commercialization of a sport, enabling players to get contracts with teams or sponsorship deals. The Olympics can be a significant step to achieving this because of the international prestige and financial support of governments. Olympic status has undoubtedly already boosted 3x3's credibility, and it will increase it further after the 2020 Tokyo games.

In 2012, during the World Tour's debut season, it was all so fresh, and teams were newly formed. The World Tour season consisted of only few events and was extremely short, lasting only three months. At that time professional basketball players could easily transition from one basketball discipline to another; however, a longer 3x3 competition season, which lasted for eight months in 2019 season, has started to change this. Now the 3x3 professional players need to dedicate themselves totally to the 3x3 game. Things developed quickly after 2014, with private organizers starting professional 3x3 leagues worldwide, such as 3x3.EXE Premier. The number of competitions grew, and the game itself exploded through increased media coverage after the IOC fulfilled 3x3's Olympic dreams in 2017. This led to the emergence of many 3x3 professional teams and leagues—a trend that continues upward today. In 2019, there were more than five thousand organized 3x3 events worldwide, and prize money increased notably with the 2019 World Tour season doubling the remuneration of the previous year.

Even after a successful first decade, FIBA has continued to set high goals and aimed to further professionalize teams, increase prize pools at events, and expand the season's duration. There were around 20 Pro Circuit events and 30 qualifiers in 2014; in 2019 there were 50 Pro Circuit events and over 100 qualifiers. FIBA 3x3 started funding travel allowances for the best 3x3 teams so they could compete at the big events, and it began handing out bonuses at the season's end. All this helped separate amateur and professional teams, who had different motivations.

While some teams are motivated by professional incentives, others just want to play for the sheer joy of the game, and organizers also welcome these entrants. Differences in motivation and professionalization meant that the gap in skill level during tournaments has widened. This has led to separate categories within tournaments based on a team's skill level and professional status. Grassroots tournaments around the world now offer two different categories for senior players: amateur and professional.

The professionalization of 3x3 will continue to shape and influence its sporting landscape, and hopes are high that further commercialization as a result of an exciting Olympic debut and the increased popularity of the World Tour will help 3x3 truly explode as a mainstream sport worldwide. The professionalization is obviously still not at the level of traditional basketball, but the future of 3x3 looks extremely bright in light of the rapid growth of its first decade.

THE ORGANIZATIONAL MODEL OF PROFESSIONAL 3X3 LEAGUES

3x3 leagues around the world are organized differently from basketball leagues, as the constitution of each league determines its nature. The NBA, for example, is a fully self-managed multi-entity league (organization) working independently of USA Basketball (the national federation). Members of the league are so-called "franchises"—anonymous societies combined to form a giant holding company. This is similar to other North American professional sports leagues, which are comprised of a stipulated number of teams, called franchises. In contrast, some European and other international basketball leagues are organized as "clubs associations." Those leagues can be run by national basketball federations. Players sign contracts with clubs, with the only link in this case being between the player and the club—unlike the NBA, where players are also tied to the league.

3x3 is different. First, "private" professional leagues host multiple tournaments. The organizational model and contract model differ across the leagues, as every private professional league has its own constitution. The 3x3.EXE Premier—the first and biggest international professional 3x3 league—is a multi-entity league with a team ownership system. It is unique because unlike the NBA, 3x3 leagues do not have a closed system in which existing franchises first must approve expansion and the incorporation of new franchises. This has allowed 3x3.EXE Premier to expand the number of teams, conferences, and countries involved every year. To compete, a team owner only needs to apply and pay a fee to the league at the beginning of every season. The average annual expense to run a 3x3 professional team in this league is around $50,000 USD.

3x3.EXE Premier also uses a different contract model compared to the NBA, which holds exclusive rights to every contract signed at the national level. This means contracts are signed with the NBA, which then gives franchises the responsibility of paying the salary stipulated in the contract. This differs to 3x3.EXE Premier's model, in which players first sign a contract with the league, where the league itself pays a player's monthly salary based on his or her team's final position at each event and on the player's individual accomplishments. Besides signing with the league, the best players also sign another contract directly with the team which generates extra yearly or monthly salaries.

THE ORGANIZATIONAL MODEL OF TEAMS ON THE FIBA 3X3 PRO CIRCUIT

Overall, professional 3x3 teams' business organization is more informal than traditional basketball teams' organization, but the number of professional 3x3 teams acting as legal entities is rising. Nevertheless, teams participating on the FIBA 3x3 World Tour do not need to be formed as a club, have a legal entity, or be part of a basketball federation or any other organization in order to be allowed to compete. How teams are organized is left completely up to the teams. In traditional basketball, a team must be formed as a legal entity, such as a club, franchise, or company, and be part of a national basketball federation or other organization in order to compete. The business organization of amateur 3x3 teams is more informal than that of the professional teams, but both can compete at the biggest FIBA 3x3 events.

The 3x3 Player Market and Contract Model

The 3x3 player market is open, and players can move freely between teams when playing at grassroots tournaments. But on the Pro Circuit, players can only play on one team per season.

The 3x3 contract model and how a player obtains his earnings strongly differs from traditional basketball as salaries for professional 3x3 players can vary wildly. Currently, top traditional basketball players earn far more than top 3x3 players, but the gap is getting smaller each year. Looking back, from 2012 until 2014, 3x3 professional players were only paid based on their individual and team successes at each 3x3 event. Teams earned monetary awards, paid by organizers, based on the final standing in each 3x3 event. The higher the final standing, the more money a team earned. This pushes 3x3 teams to play at numerous events where only high final standings guarantees them high earnings. However, professionalism has progressed, and these days, the best 3x3 professional players sign a contract with a team, company, or a team owner at the start of each season, guaranteeing them a yearly salary. Furthermore, 3x3 players are paid by event organizers, such as professional leagues or FIBA 3x3, based on the team's final standing at each event. Last but not least, FIBA 3x3 pays annual bonuses to the best teams at the end of a season. This means that the 3x3 contract model strongly differs from basketball's where most players have fixed yearly salaries.

Novi Sad Al Wahda: The Model Professional Team

The undisputed 3x3 powerhouse Novi Sad Al Wahda and its superstar players, who have represented Serbia and the UAE at global events, is the model professional 3x3 team. Among their notable achievements, they are four-time World Cup champions, four-time World Tour champions, and two-time Europe Cup champions. In their historic 2018 season, they won all three cups, finishing with an incredible 42 wins and 0 losses across those events.

They began their dynasty in 2012 as simply Novi Sad when they won the first FIBA 3x3 World Cup. At the start of the 2015 season, they found sponsorship in the UAE and changed their name to Novi Sad Al Wahda. Other teams quickly followed Novi Sad's lead and went professional, leading to a battle for supremacy over 3x3's crown. To everyone's surprise, the most successful 3x3 team broke up before the start of the 2021 World Tour season. The team has mainly consisted of Dušan Domović Bulut, Dejan Majstorović, Tamás Ivosev, Marko Ždero, and Marko Savić—all of whom except for Ivosev played for the Serbian national team.

3x3 Novi Sad team from left to right: Dušan Bulut, Dejan Majstorović, Marko Savić, and Tamas Ivosev.

Team Serbia has clashed with team USA multiple times over the years and famously won the 2016 World Cup final against the Americans with a score of 21-16.

An Interview with Dušan Domović Bulut

Dušan Domović Bulut has been the star player for Novi Sad since the team's formation in 2012 and is arguably 3x3's GOAT—demonstrated by his being a two-time World Tour and World Cup MVP whose team has seen unparalleled success. For the first book on the sport, Bulut—affectionately known as Mr. Bulutproof to fans—just had to be interviewed.

Dušan, how do you remember the early years?

When we started playing 3x3, we were young, extremely motivated, and we always had a desire to be the best. We quickly learned that we have to put in the hard work to achieve what we want. I remember our start fondly, but it was certainly difficult as 3x3 was not yet internationally recognized, and prizes on the events were not as high as they are now. At that time, we decided to invest the money we earned back into the team in a bid to further progress. We started without a coach, but with our prize money, we were able to afford one and later add more staff each year. This enabled us to train properly and only specifically for 3x3. Besides coaching, we also invested our earnings into marketing as well as medical and other services. We were continually looking to progress, and it all led to championships and a sponsorship from Al Wahda.

What is the difference between a traditional player and 3x3 player?

3x3 players need to be able to carry more responsibilities within a team, and the game itself is mentally more demanding. Mental concentration and self-discipline for our team were crucial for sustained success. Especially, being mentally prepared at the start of the game is extremely important since a game lasts only 10 minutes. Before the game, I warm up first and then I mentally prepare. I move into my own world and think about the game and visualize the plays that will or might happen during the game. If we are talking about differences off the court, I think it's important to mention that in 3x3, you are not given anything, because you have to repeatedly prove yourself every game and every event. You are paid based on current results and final standing at each event, but basketball players are paid on talent and previous results.

Dušan Domović Bulut

How was your team formed, and what were your team's traits?

In all those years and as we were winning multiple championships, we were extremely disciplined and hungry for more, so it's fair to say that my teammates' best traits were their dedication to the success of the team and willingness to sacrifice. We were most dominant in transition offense, and this was by far our biggest advantage over opponents. We also had well-distributed roles in the team. Dejan was a great two-point shooter, moved great without the ball, and had a winner's mentality. He hated losing. Marko [Savić] was an all-around player and the playmaker of our team, who understood the game perfectly and made his teammates better. Tamás brought great energy, was dominant under the basket, and most important he was able to guard different types of players. He was a typical center in basketball. We added him to our roster later on, when Ždero was getting older, as he was an upgraded version of Ždero who was also such a great defensive player and brought a lot of energy to the team.

What is your advantage over other 3x3 players?

My mindset both on and off the court. I have always had the motivation and desire to be the best and to win, but I had to work hard and stay focused on the goal through many seasons, even though it was hard sometimes, and many would stop. You know there wasn't as much money in 3x3 at the beginning as there is now. On the court I love to have ball in my hands, and I feel born to take the last shot which decided the winner. I'm not the best athlete myself. I'm not the fastest. I'm not the best shooter. But I've developed an all-around game which is necessary in 3x3. At the end of the day, you have to love what you do if you want to be successful. I can honestly say I love 3x3. I enjoy playing it just for fun with friends or professionally. This game is my life.

THE 3X3 COMPETITION SEASON

3x3 is played year round, with events staged both indoors and outdoors depending on weather conditions. Most 3x3 events are organized outdoors in the Northern Hemisphere's summer and during the traditional basketball off-season. But since 2014, the FIBA 3x3 World Tour has gradually expanded and started encroaching into the basketball season. With 3x3's popularity increasing, some national basketball federations and private promoters have also begun to organize 3x3 leagues, event tours, and single tournaments during the traditional basketball season, making it difficult or even impossible for players to effectively compete in both disciplines.

How to Climb World Rankings

To climb the ladder of world rankings, each team has to carefully plan its season. If players were just introduced to 3x3 and they have big plans in this basketball discipline the plan should be as follows: First, players or coaches need to carefully select their events on play.fiba3x3.com before the season starts. They need to understand the hierarchy of the FIBA 3x3 competition network where one qualifier leads to the next event, and if successful a team, can play on the World Tour. The planning before the season is vital because there isn't a fixed schedule of games for a team as in traditional basketball, and the level of events can vary. A plan might need to be adjusted mid-season to accommodate shifting goals based on success in qualifiers. For a team to have a chance to be among the highest ranked teams in the world, they have to attend at least nine high-level events in one season (level 7 and up).

3x3 Training

The furious pace of 3x3 puts demands on players' cardiovascular, respiratory, neuromuscular, and other functional systems. Preparing well is vital for handling the rigors of a hectic schedule that tests players both physically and mentally. With so many games thrown into such short events—often lasting just two days—3x3 players need to be in shape. A team should always strive for progress and set a long-term training plan using periodization, which systematically divides an annual training plan into specific time blocks. The goal is to maximize team and player performance, which requires finding the right training volume and intensity. Moreover, proper periodization ensures that a player reaches full potential during the most important part of the season. Numerous factors are involved in setting a proper periodization plan, including the competition calendar, an athlete's ability and potential, and whether a player plays only 3x3 or plays traditional basketball too.[35]

When the World Tour was first established, players mostly trained with scrimmage drills, which improve conditioning, fitness, and technique while sharpening team tactics and building chemistry. There wasn't as much emphasis on individual coaching. But this has changed now that teams have started to employ specialized staffs. As teams start gaining more resources, they continued adding specialists to further develop the players.

Because 3x3 is a high-intensity sport, training should be similarly high-intensity to reflect game situations. High-intensity interval training (HIIT) programs are suitable because they include sudden bursts of high-intensity activity akin to a 3x3 game. For professional 3x3 players, a 2:1 work-to-rest ratio is beneficial, with intensity at or close to maximal effort.[33] Rest is also an integral part of a 3x3 season. Though it can sometimes be overlooked, it is vital for athletes and particularly important in 3x3, where players' bodies can take a pounding during games.

Training Phases for a 3x3 Season

A 3x3 training plan should include preparatory, competition, and transition phases. Teams need to prepare their calendars to ensure the right amount of training (loading and unloading the volume and intensity) in each phase and avoid injuries and excessive stress on the body. Teams physically prepare and set goals for the competition season during the preparatory phase, which lasts from the end of the previous season's transition phase until the beginning of competition. If players don't prepare well, they may start the season slow or become injured. In the competition phase, teams are competing in events and need the right management of high-level performance through macrocycles of loading and unloading. A transition period offers players respite after the season and a welcome opportunity to recover.[35]

Warming Up and Preventing Injuries

Playing a high-intensity and physical game, particularly when the stakes are high, can lead to injuries. Low-body injuries are far more common than upper body. Lots of jumping and rapid changes of direction put immense pressure on knees and tendons and ligaments in the legs. To decrease the risks of low-body injuries, players should develop and maintain a strengthening program involving exercises that target muscles in the legs, glutes, ankles, and core. To further minimalize risks of injuries, 3x3 players need to properly warm up and stretch before each game, but be aware 3x3 professional teams are usually only granted three to five minutes for a warm-up on the court before the game, whereas in basketball it can be more than an hour. So, it is extremely important for an athlete to be disciplined and make a dynamic stretching warm-up before he even steps on the court.

Traveling

3x3 teams do not have the privilege of home games at team arenas. They have to keep a tough travel schedule to play on the circuit. Events are held every week worldwide—many played in far-flung locations, requiring constant long-distance travel and time changes, which represent additional stress for athletes and their bodies. 3x3 events last only a few days before players have to abruptly leave for the next event, which might be held on a different continent. Jet lag, which is the result of the body's circadian rhythms not being aligned with the local time, leads to issues such as a disrupted sleep cycle and lack of energy. The ability to adjust and prepare for these changes is essential for a 3x3 player to maintain a top-level performance.

Can a Player Engage Professionally in Both Disciplines?

With the World Tour growing longer over the years, top professional 3x3 players have faced heavier workloads, making it harder now to engage professionally in both 3x3 and traditional basketball. The men's professional basketball season in most parts of the world lasts from October to April or May, while the 2019

FIBA 3x3 World Tour ran from April to November. The periodization of these two disciplines do not match, and competition period for both lasts too long for players to fully play both, with the seasons briefly overlapping twice a year. If a player wants to fully professionalize in both disciplines, suitable preparation would not really be possible, because the preparation phase for 3x3 training would be during basketball's competition season. The transition period, when players recover physically and mentally, would be non-existent.[35] The risk of injuries would thus increases sharply, likely resulting in an accumulation of micro traumas and making chronic injuries inevitable.

However, for players who only play in privately organized professional 3x3 leagues, it may be easier to practice both disciplines, as those leagues are usually only organized during basketball's off-season and last only a few months. Preferably, players should prioritize one of the games while perhaps going semi-pro or amateur in the other. Pro players are left with a daunting choice: 3x3 or traditional basketball?

Table 25: The number of games played (GP) and the number games played on the Pro Circuit and in national team competitions (ProC + NT) per season by Dejan Majstorović of Novi Sad

Year	2015	2016	2017	2018	2019
GP	77	100	109	101	100
ProC + NT	38	59	81	70	85
Duration	May–Oct	June–Oct	April–Oct	April–Oct	April–Nov

PROFESSIONAL 3X3 PLAYERS

3x3's evolving professionalization has enticed elite athletes to pursue the game. Current 3x3 professionals play more games in a season than NBA players. They have to be mentally, physically, technically, and tactically prepared for the particular demands of the sport, which can take years to fully understand and master.

Table 26: Number of games played (GP) in a season by 3x3 professionals in 2019

Name	Team	GP
Nauris Miezis	Riga (LAT)	115
Marko Savić	Novi Sad (SRB)	103
Mihailo Vasić	Liman (SRB)	102
Robbie Hummel	Princeton (USA)	78

Table 27: Number of games played (GP) by NBA players in the 2018/2019 season and postseason

Name	Team	GP
Stephen Curry	Golden State Warriors	91
Giannis Antetokounmpo	Milwaukee Bucks	87
Kawhi Leonard	Toronto Raptors	84
Lebron James	Los Angeles Lakers	55

A Sport Without Positions

3x3 is a positionless sport; the official 3x3 rules don't specify set positions for players. It is also impractical to have defined positions in 3x3 because players are expected to carry out numerous roles and move all over the court constantly within a short period. However, not every player is equally good at everything, so players do have specific roles in a team's tactics in order to take advantage of their best traits and skills. The style of play of the modern 3x3 professional teams is most similar to traditional basketball style of play called "small ball." This style of play is popular in the NBA where size and low-post play are sacrificed in favor of speed, agility, and three-point shooting. Teams believe that the right combination of speed and shooting can beat size.

Pioneering 3x3 Players and Their Transition to 3x3

In the first decade of 3x3, teams experienced less access to support staff compared to their counterparts in traditional basketball. Pioneering 3x3 players therefore had more responsibilities and had to make more decisions, both on and off the court.

The most successful 3x3 players of the first decade were the ones who had transitioned from traditional basketball. However, they needed to adapt to 3x3's rule and nuances. Experience also played a vital role in past World Tours during which experienced and older teams were more successful. Younger teams or younger players (u-21) were simply not as dominant because they needed to first mature both tactically and physically in order to be able to successfully compete in this intense and physical basketball discipline. Looking at what type of basketball players generally became 3x3 professionals, we can see that size and shape was a huge factor, leading to shooting guards or forwards being highly represented. Players from these positions generally have the skills 3x3 demands: speed, agility, and shooting capacity, while still being able to maintain physical strength and contest rebound shots.[36] However, players from these positions encountered some fundamental changes as they transitioned to 3x3.

The Point Guard

A point guard in traditional basketball usually brings the ball up the court, calls plays, and is most often the team's shortest player and best passer. He or she is the person most often in charge of the ball. Point guards' skill sets are broad, but their anthropometric characteristics (weight and height) are often not ideal for 3x3's switching defense. A guard transitioning to 3x3 will be initially surprised with:

★ having to defend bigger and stronger opponents in the transition phase;

★ the higher level of physicality and the constant fight not to be out-positioned;

★ not having the ball in hands as often and not initiating all of the offenses, as this responsibility is more equally divided between the players.

To be successful on offense, a point guard will be forced to crash the offensive glass more frequently (rather than protecting the fast break) and make more off- and on-ball screens than in traditional basketball.

The Small Forward

Small forwards are highly sought after in 3x3 because of their size and versatility. A small forward with the characteristics of a "two-way 3 and D player," a "two-way 3-level scorer," or any other two-way versatile player is generally the ideal 3x3 player. These players can do it all—handle the ball, make plays, shoot from range, and play in the post. They are usually good rebounders and versatile defenders of a decent size. Apart from shooting guards, small forwards have the skill set that translates most readily to 3x3.

The Center

The basketball center is the tallest player on the team. Centers might not be agile, but they are able to set good screens, dominate under the basket offensively and defensively, and rebound proficiently. Big players transitioning into 3x3 might experience difficulties guarding smaller and quicker players. The speed, agility, quick changes of direction, and constant movements of 3x3 are a big change. Centers in basketball often make up for their lack of agility and technical skills with their height or strength, but those deficiencies are harder to cover up in 3x3. Moreover, savvy 3x3 teams use denial defense in transition to make these big players dribble once they rebound and force them outside the two-point arc, where they are not comfortable, as they are not used to initiating offense or shooting and driving from behind the three-point line in traditional basketball. Centers have thus found it more difficult than other players to adapt to 3x3, and they have been a minority in the first decade. Those who have transitioned have needed to fine tune their game to be successful.

The Characteristics of Professional 3x3 Players

What are the skills that a professional 3x3 player needs to develop? What characteristics have defined a professional 3x3 player in the first decade of 3x3's existence?

Anthropometric Characteristics

Comparing statistics from the 2019 3x3 and NBA seasons, it's safe to say that professional 3x3 players are smaller on average than traditional basketballers. Most notably, 3x3 lacks extremely tall players (the centers in traditional basketball) and very small players (who often play point guards in traditional basketball). This is not to say, however, that these players can't make it in 3x3. Anyone with the skills, savvy, and desire can succeed. But versatility is a 3x3 team's most-coveted attribute. Research has shown that extra height and aerobic capacity may be less of an advantage in 3x3 compared to traditional basketball, with speed and agility in a confined playing space deemed as more important.[33]

Research by P. Montgomery and B. Maloney conducted at a series of FIBA 3x3 competitions with more than two hundred 3x3 National Team and World Tour players found that the body size and shape of male professional 3x3 players was most similar to forwards (perimeter wing players) in traditional basketball; they matched the height and weight characteristics, but they had greater body mass. Generally, female players were most similar to guards.[33]

Motor and Functional Skills

3x3 professionals need to maintain and improve motor and functional abilities through strength, speed, coordination, agility, mobility, and endurance training, among others. These kinds of training will help develop the skills needed for players to quickly and efficiently move around the court and promptly recover between periods. Moreover, due to the high physicality of 3x3, players should improve their strength, power, and stability, which will help them sustain physical contact and enable them to achieve optimal performance. Physically strong players are at an advantage because their physicality can stymie quicker players. With more contact, holding, and pushing prevalent in 3x3 than in traditional basketball (where referees will blow the whistle and call a foul on even the slightest contact), strong offensive players can carve out more space and a better position for an offensive rebound while strong defenders can limit penetration to the basket.

3x3 requires high-speed inertial movements within a limited space, creating a relatively high physiological response.[37] This includes many accelerations and decelerations, shuffling, rapid direction changes and jumps, all within a confined playing arena. Therefore, exceptional motor skills, quick acceleration and deceleration, quick changes of directions, power, and high jumping ability will help players succeed in 3x3. While in traditional basketball, developing a maximum running speed is important because players tend to run longer distances (from one basket to another), in 3x3, explosive speed and agility enabling quick and efficient changes of directions are far more important since the court is much shorter.

Mental Skills

Mental skills are of the utmost importance in 3x3 due to a player's in-game independence and increased responsibility compared to traditional basketball. In a game with no coach on the sideline, teams require an on-court leader to fill the gap. Therefore, leadership qualities and selfless behavior are important traits in a quality 3x3 player. Because games only last for 10 minutes or less and the transitions from defense to offense happen very quickly, it is important for players to maintain concentration for every possession. A player's quick anticipation, reaction, and decision-making, with good improvisation and intuition, are more necessary for success than in traditional basketball.

With in-game coaching not allowed, 3x3 players have to solve problems instinctively, making teamwork extremely important, with players communicating verbally or through hand signs. These cues have to be executed at the right time; fouling or misusing time-out might be the difference between winning and losing. Therefore, in order to successfully cope with these tactical difficulties, players need to completely understand the game and develop high basketball IQ.

A player's mindset is the precursor to effort and intensity and extremely important because qualities such as determination, work rate, toughness, hustle, discipline, sense of space, and aggressiveness together make a great 3x3 player. (Sense of space is vital because of the lack of players on the court. Knowing where a ball will bounce after a missed basket is an important intangible.) Although 3x3 is played by a small number of players, the psycho-social aspect is evident. Players need to develop a great team chemistry and other social skills. These are critical given the amount of time teams spend together.

Decision-Making, Court Awareness, and Counting Possessions

Court awareness and counting possessions enables better decision-making. Players can develop these skills through experience and training. Many 3x3 games go down to the wire, and a player's ability to calculate how many possessions are left is critical.

If there are an average of 35 possessions per 10-minutes World Tour game, teams have 3.5 possessions on average per minute. How many possessions a team has depends on the pace of that particular game. If a team is behind by two points with one minute left and players know there are three possessions or more left in the game, they can go for a one-pointer instead of forcing twos and going for broke because there is still time to play it safe.

For example, with a team up 14-9 with two minutes of regular time left, there should be, in theory—depending on the game's pace—seven possessions or more remaining for each team. Teams leading at this interval do not want opponents shooting two-pointers, and their strategy should be to slow the tempo, not take risky shots, and tighten up defensively. An opposing team would need five one-pointers from seven or more remaining possessions to tie the game. Their percentage of one-point shots would need to be 70 percent, which is difficult to achieve. It all means that teams leading from this position should win, so long as they make right decisions.

3x3, however, can turn in seconds, and if the trailing team scores consecutive twos, then they are back in the game. At 14-13 with 1.5 minutes left, each team might have five possessions remaining. Players have to be aware of the possessions left and the strategies involved—something resembling a chess match. Two-pointers in 3x3 are so important—even more than in basketball because they are worth double the alternative. It's why professional teams purposely give opponents an easy basket for one instead of letting them attempt a two. Having good tactics—and knowing when to use them—is vital, and players always need to be switched on, because it can decide the outcome of the game.

What Factors In to a Player's In-Game Decision-Making?

All decisions in 3x3 come with risks. Nothing is certain in a competitive game, where situations are ambiguous and execution depends on teamwork.

To date, professional 3x3 teams have averaged more than 30 possessions per game. Rational decisions in each possession are what lead to success. The five fundamental factors that affect a 3x3 player's in-game decisions are time, space, personal fouls, score, and outside conditions.

Special Basketball Skills

Special basketball skills are those abilities such as shooting, passing, and dribbling that require gaining, maintaining, and adapting various motor skills. Because of the limited number of players on a team, professional 3x3 players need a versatile offensive and defensive skill set with few deficiencies; otherwise, they will be exploited—and possibly made into a meme. Ideally, professional 3x3 players should be capable of executing every task on offense, even if they mainly stick with what they are best at. Versatility is particularly treasured, but players can carve out a niche through a specialist skill such as two-point shooting. Not every player can be flawless, but successful teams can cover those deficiencies. The special basketball skills a player needs to obtain in order to be successful are presented in more detail in the chapters 7, 8, and 9.

Types of 3x3 Players

First Classification

The first classification divides 3x3 players into three basic types, distinguished by player skill set: one-dimensional players, multi-dimensional players, and pan-dimensional players. Since 3x3 is positionless, a player's ability to successfully fill different roles tends to define that player.

One-dimensional players are specialists who have specific roles for their teams. They usually excel in one skill and are common in basketball, but not so much in 3x3. Because they don't have well-rounded skills sets, team strategies need to be able to cover their weaknesses.

Multi-dimensional players can attack and defend most opponents efficiently. They have a broader skill set than one-dimensional players and can execute most tasks.

Pan-dimensional players have the broadest skill set, allowing them to efficiently defend and attack virtually any opponent. They can assist, dribble, and score inside and outside, and they don't have any specific deficiencies in their game. Pan-dimensional players and multi-dimensional players tend to be more suitable for professional competitions than one-dimensional players.

While roles might be different in 3x3 and traditional basketball, the ultimate goal of creating synergy both offensively and defensively remains the same in both games.

Second Classification

The second classification divide players into one-way and two-way players depending on how successfully they can perform specific tasks in a single game phase.

A two-way player excels at both offense and defense. This is the ideal 3x3 player. Not every NBA player excels at a two-way game; many are specialists or much better on either offense or defense. But most of the absolute elite are good at both, including Giannis Antetokounmpo, Jimmy Butler, Anthony Davis, and Kawhi Leonard, among others.

In 3x3, after a scored basket, the play is live, and players don't have time to choose one person to guard but have to guard whoever is closest. This means they have to defend multiple players throughout a game. By contrast, the fact that traditional basketball is played on two baskets means basketball players have time to find their designated opponents while the team sets up the defense. 3x3's fast transition phase makes it critical for teams to have two-way players who can't be easily exploited in mismatches.

Versatile Two-Way Players

When a basketball team forms, the decision-makers first look for elite players such as Luka Dončić whom they can build a team around. These players will have the biggest usage rate on the team—the percentage of team plays used by a player while he was on the floor. Later, decision-makers add other high caliber players and "role players"—that is, players with a specific skill set—to round out the team. Role players are usually great three-point shooters, rebounders, or blockers. They are sometimes versatile two-way players, but not always. They do not need to excel in every task because a basketball coach can deploy tasks between five different players. If having a versatile two-way player on a traditional basketball roster is a bonus, then it is a necessity in 3x3.

3x3 teams follow basketball's blueprint, but highly skilled and versatile two-way players are more valuable in this format where every skill of the game is exposed. 3x3's quick transitions, 12 seconds on the shot clock, and the fact there are only three players on a team force all players to constantly pass, drive, dribble, shoot inside and outside, rebound, and switch, making versatility and high "basketball IQ" essential. Those who lack any of the aforementioned skills will be quickly exposed. 3x3 players who are able to efficiently guard multiple types of players and efficiently execute multiple tasks on offense are worth their weight in gold.

Hiding Deficiencies and the Importance of Quality Teammates

Traditional basketball can often make up for an underperforming player or two, given that they can be covered on defense and effectively shut out of the offense.

But in the uncompromising world of 3x3 the weakest link is brutally attacked both on offense and defense. Deficiencies are frequently exposed, and even one subpar player on a team can stand out like a sore thumb—much more than in traditional basketball. For a team to succeed, it needs four quality players.

The weakest link is brutally attacked on defense because he doesn't have anywhere to hide on the court. It is risky for a teammate to stack the paint or implement a deep help defense due to the open space. All this leads to something fans are not used to in traditional basketball: 3x3 professionals choose not to help with cover if the primary defender gets overrun, electing to give uncontested layups rather than opening the way for a two-pointer. It is also worth noting that transition phase frequently forces defensive players to switch, creating mismatches and reinforcing the importance of one-on-one defense.

On offense, there is more equality among players, but this means offensive weaknesses can be ruthlessly exposed. Notably, those who can't shoot can be left alone behind the arc. All this reinforces the importance of each individual who needs to have as few deficiencies as possible while possessing great or adequate ball-handling, shooting, rebounding, and other skills on defense and offense. There is already an adage in 3x3 that rings true: The team is only as strong as its weakest link.

The Value of Less-Known NBA Players in 3x3

Many people have wondered which basketball players would thrive in 3x3. We have already partly answered that question. Simply put, a highly skilled two-way versatile player who has a high "basketball IQ" is ideal in 3x3 and has enormous value. It is clear that NBA stars such as Luka Dončić, LeBron James, Kawhi Leonard, and Anthony Davis would thrive in 3x3. LeBron James has said his all-time 3x3 team would include himself, Magic Johnson, and Michael Jordan.[22] Quite obviously, that team would destroy their opponents, considering they are three of the greatest to ever play hoops. But it's even more intriguing to consider which lesser-known players would thrive in the 3x3 format. For this thought experiment, I only considered NBA players who had a career average of at most nine points per game prior to the 2020–2021 NBA season.

Jerami Grant, who is a "stretch four" player, OG Anunoby, who is a "3 and D" player, and Mikal Bridges all don't have a high usage percentage in the NBA and are not "ball dominant" players, but they are versatile two-way players who would probably have had more value and appeal in 3x3. Another such player is Will Clyburn, who thrives in Europe and has a similar style, allowing him to cover more space. Those versatile players can score inside (on low post), drive, shoot threes efficiently, defend effectively, and guard different types of players with their huge wingspans. They are also agile and can space the floor (that it, they have good off-ball movement), assist, dribble, share, and handle the ball adequately—an ideal skill set for 3x3.

On the other hand, basketball centers have had the most problems transitioning to 3x3. The best 3x3 players resembling centers in traditional basketball have been Tamás Ivosev, Kareem Maddox, and Marcel Esonwune, who are all extremely agile and have a great footwork for their size. They all have defensive versatility, physicality, and good rim protection, while each has a different skill set on offense. Bam Adebayo is an excellent example of a so-called center who would be a good fit on a 3x3 team. He had a low career average of 10.5 points per game prior to the 2020–2021 NBA season and is quickly blossoming, as indicated by his becoming an All-Star in 2020, so he doesn't technically qualify for this exercise by the rules I've set for myself. His three-point percentage is low, but he compensates for that by being agile and an elite defender who can guard almost anyone. On offense, he can organize, assist, drive, move nicely without the ball, screen, and score.

The Fundamental Skill Set of 3x3

The 3x3 skill set, also called player technique, is the set of movements with or without the ball in accordance with rules that are tactically effective. While playing games and executing these skills, players should always strive to take advantage of their unique abilities and characteristics.[29] The fundamental skills are basic technical skills, such as jumping, dribbling, and passing, and they are the same in 3x3 as in basketball. They can be divided into two primary categories: offensive skills such as shooting or passing and defensive skills such as blocking or stealing. It is extremely important, for younger players especially, to practice and develop these skills. However, a 3x3 player with poor technique—such as poor ball handling skills—can still be dominant and useful to a team by being physically dominant, which is an important feature in 3x3.

Most of the fundamental 3x3 skills can be performed in low or in high stance, and one of the unique characteristics of 3x3 is that professional players spend more time in a low stance compared to traditional basketball players. Low basketball stance has certain advantages for a player without the ball, as it enables fast movement and quick changes of direction. For a dribbler, it enables faster dribbling and movement, better control, and more hand contact with the ball.

Some more complex technical-tactical elements—or "two-man" offensive plays such as the pick and roll, pick and pop, or handoffs—can be executed differently in 3x3 than in traditional basketball due to the differing rules. Professional 3x3 players thus need a slightly different set of skills from traditional basketball players when they are executing complex techniques. We will get to know the usefulness and value of these plays in chapters 8 and 9.

Developing Youth in 3x3

At the professional level of 3x3, winning is important. But the primary reason for kids to play should be enjoyment. Since it is predominantly a summer game, kids can play 3x3 during a part of the year when they can be more focused on recreation. Summer provides a lot of flexibility for kids to play 3x3 since it is a traditionally less hectic season.

Generally, there are not a lot of big differences in training between traditional basketball and 3x3 for players younger than 15 since basic skills are the same in both disciplines. Thus, players can freely transition between disciplines. But there is one big difference which should be noted: youth who want to play 3x3 later on at senior professional competitions should develop the skills sets needed for positionless basketball. This means that younger players should develop all of the game's skills. In traditional basketball, sometimes coaches will stereotype younger players and set training based on their future positions.

Importantly, the transition from aerobic to anaerobic activity has to be gradual for youth, and they have to first sufficiently develop their basic skill sets before they train for the specific and more complex nuances of 3x3.

PROFESSIONAL COACHING

Unlike in traditional basketball, where a game in some leagues can't start without a licensed coach on each team, 3x3 teams didn't and still don't have to have a coach to compete at FIBA 3x3 events. How a team is organized is left completely to the team. A 3x3 team can play on the Pro Circuit whether they consist of players only, of players and a coach, or of players, a coach, and other specialized staff people. When the World Tour started in 2012, teams had no support staff, but after 2015, teams beefed up their staffs, and soon coaches became 3x3 specialists as the game evolved tactically.

Danilo Lukić: A Pioneering Coach

In order to completely understand the work of the 3x3 professional coach, it's only fair to take the coach of the most dominant and successful 3x3 team ever as an example. Novi Sad's coach from 2015 to 2020 was Danilo Lukić. As a coach, Lukić focused on training and coaching the team before the event and then traveling with them for the competitions. During events, he was responsible for scouting opponents and physically, mentally, and tactically preparing the team between games.

I interviewed Mr. Lukić to see how the multi-time World Cup and World Tour champs operated. Here's what he told me:

> Our way of operating was unique. We basically made all the important decisions about the gameplay together as a team, such as how we would play and the tactics involved, meaning that apart from training, I didn't have as strict authority over the team as coaches normally have in basketball. As a team, we also talked a lot about how we can further develop, and we always functioned like that—looking for mutual team

consensus. I think in order to have success in 3x3, all players have to be on the same page, have the same vision, and have great team chemistry. Our team had all that. On the court players also complemented each other perfectly because they had well-assigned roles, which formed a great mosaic. However, every 3x3 team needs a leader, and Dušan Bulut was a great leader of our team. During my coaching career and especially at the start with 3x3 Novi Sad, I experienced different roles. I was strength and conditioning coach, one-on-one trainer so each player could develop his basketball skills, and I also develop and set team strategies. Basically, I lead and had all the authority on practices, where I set training drills that would help the team further progress their skills, tactics and other things. At the events, I offered the team support with physical warm-ups, tactical and mental preparation, and scout reports if we didn't know the opposition. Then we sat down as a team, and we discussed what would be the best options to play on defense and offense. If there was any doubt, Dušan Bulut's thinking prevailed, as he was well prepared, organized, and had great knowledge about the game and opposing players. Lastly, I think it is vital for a coach to keep team spirits high, because 3x3 is mentally very demanding, and you also spend a lot of time together with players on the road. The way we operated, by giving players certain freedom and not having as strict authority as in basketball apart from practices, was a good thing, in my opinion, because what matters in sport are results, and ours showed that.[38]

The Coach's Role

The main task of a 3x3 coach is to instruct, train, and prepare players during practice sessions so they are able to properly and efficiently execute the coach's philosophy, tactics, and tasks in game without the aid of in-game coaching. Clearly, the best 3x3 coaches have enormous impact on both players and the team gameplay. Even though they may be out of sight during games, their imprint is always noticeable. Other important coaching tasks include clearly setting player roles, being aware of team strengths and weaknesses, and formulating tactics and principles in training to help the team keep improving. These tasks are important because, for a team to be successful, every player must understand and accept his or her role.

Traditional basketball coaches obviously have more of a role during games, but their 3x3 counterparts have a greater responsibility off the court and undergo a greater burden if they don't have a support staff. Because they had fewer resources, the first 3x3 coaches had the dual role of coach-manager, in contrast to traditional basketball coaches. The extra duties meant 3x3 coaches planned, organized, lead, coordinated, and controlled an entire team.

Like any leader, 3x3 coaches need to be able to connect and motivate in a bid to inspire their players. They have to be clear about team goals, finding the right balance when forming teams and fostering chemistry. Ideally, they need to know 3x3 inside and out and continually transfer that knowledge to the players.

The Coach's Role at Events

Don't misunderstand; a 3x3 coach still has a big role at events despite the fact he is not allowed to coach during the games. At events, a 3x3 coach should be a role model for players, support a team from the stands, harness team chemistry, analyze the opposition, and mentally, physically, and tactically prepare a team before each game. Lastly, after each game, he should advise and coach players while being honest and objective.

Professional Development for Coaches

3x3's profile has risen quickly, marked by its Olympic status, but there have been no coaching certificate programs in 3x3's first decade. To date, 3x3 coaches have depended on individual research and prior basketball knowledge and experience. This might soon change. A coaching certificate program would allow coaches to further professionalize in 3x3 and be licensed, just like in traditional basketball. Undoubtedly, as 3x3 continues to grow, coaches will have more opportunities to learn, professionalize, and build up their knowledge.

CHAPTER 7
STATISTICAL ANALYSIS AND ADVANCED DATA ANALYTICS

ABBREVIATIONS

3x3 Basketball

★ 3x3 WT = 3x3 World Tour

★ 3x3 WS = 3x3 Women's Series

★ Novi Sad (SRB), Princeton (USA), Liman (SRB) and Riga (LAT) represented the best professional 3x3 teams in the world in the 2019 3x3 WT season.

As the highest level of 3x3's competition network, the World Tour was logical choice to evaluate. The data in this chapter were collected by FIBA 3x3. The advanced data calculation and analysis are the work of the author.

Traditional Basketball

★ NBA = National Basketball Association

★ LAL = Los Angeles Lakers

★ MIA = Miami Heat

★ MIL = Milwaukee Bucks

★ TOR = Toronto Raptors

★ GS = Golden State Warriors

★ CLE = Cleveland Cavaliers

★ LNB PRO A = Top French basketball league

★ ACB = Top Spanish basketball league

★ NBL = Top Australian basketball league

★ CBA = Top Chinese basketball league

★ WC = World Cup

★ EC = European Championship

Statistics relate to the regular-season averages of the respective basketball teams. The data was obtained from Basketball-Reference.com. Unavailable data points were calculated by the author.

Statistical Abbreviations and Explanations

★ PTS = Points

★ PPG = Points per game

★ GP = Games played

★ LG = Lost games

★ WG = Won games

★ WBL = Win before the regulation time has expired

★ WBL % = Games won before the regulation time has expired divided by all games played

★ FT = Free throw shot

3X3 BASKETBALL ★

- ★ 1-pt = one-point shot

- ★ 2-pt = two-point shot

- ★ 1-pt Freq % = Percentage of attempted shots that were one-point attempts

- ★ 2-pt Freq % = Percentage of attempted shots that were two-point attempts

- ★ FT Freq % = Percentage of attempted shots that were free throw attempts

- ★ %PTS FT = Percentage of points from free throws

- ★ %PTS 2-pt = Percentage of points from two-point shots

- ★ %PTS 1-pt = Percentage of points from one-point shots

- ★ OFF REB = Offensive rebound

- ★ DEF REB = Defensive rebound

- ★ TOT REB = Total rebounds

- ★ OFF REB% = Percentage of available offensive rebounds a team grabbed during the game

- ★ DEF REB% = Percentage of available defensive rebounds a team grabbed during the game

- ★ TO = Turnover

- ★ TO % = Turnover percentage

- ★ FTM = Free throw shot made

- ★ FTA = Free throw shot attempted

- ★ FT % = Free throw shot percentage

- ★ FTR= Free throw rate

- ★ FTR%= Free throw rate percentage

- ★ Freq= Frequency

- ★ 1-ptm = one-point shot made

★ 1-pta = one-point shot attempted

★ 1-pt % = one-point shot percentage

★ 2-ptm = two-point shot made

★ 2-pta = two-point shot attempted

★ 2-pt % = two-point shot percentage

★ Total shot % = Total shot percentage

★ EFG % = Effective field goal percentage = ([1-ptm + 2-ptm] × 2) / (1-pta + 2-pta)

★ %TOTSHOT= team's total shots divided by opponent's total shots, expressed as a percentage

★ BS = Blocked shot

★ KAS = Key assist

★ POSS = Possessions

★ TF = Team fouls

★ TFA = Team fouls against

★ OFF Rat = Offensive rating

★ DEF Rat = Defensive rating

★ p.p. = percentage points

★ SR = substitution rate (number of substitutions per dead-ball situation)

ADVANCED DATA ANALYTICS AND EVERYTHING YOU NEED TO KNOW ABOUT 3X3 STATS AND PLAYER EVALUATIONS

At the turn of the millennium, sports underwent an information revolution. The genesis started with "moneyball" in the early 2000s, which revolutionized the staid sport of baseball through sports analytics, using statistics and data to analyze and study teams' and players' value and efficiency. By applying mathematical and statistical principles, analytics had many off-field, but more importantly, on-field applications, including improving both individual and team performance. Numbers and sophisticated technology essentially replaced the "eye-test" of scouts and coaches, leading to a better understanding of baseball. Common beliefs and tactics were suddenly overturned by this new phenomenon, which became the subject of the hit feature film *Moneyball* in 2010 and eventually influenced other sports, including basketball.

Back in the early 2000s, it was all about spreadsheets and linear regression; however, by the early 2010s, NBA teams started hiring data analysts, and the league installed a video player-tracking system in every arena to gather an extensive database of player statistics. The tracking system, which follows the ball and every player on the court through sophisticated software, goes beyond the box score and provides valuable information such as players' top speed, distance covered and almost everything else imaginable.

NBA teams suddenly became data-driven. Owners began hiring general managers who were experts in data analysis rather than former players, who had traditionally taken these types of top roles. Perhaps the most prominent example was Daryl Morey, who never played basketball professionally but was extremely proficient with numbers and had qualifications in computer science. After becoming the general manager of the Houston Rockets in 2006, Morey was at the forefront of the advanced analytics movement and the three-point revolution—aptly called "Moreyball." In his 14-year tenure, the Rockets won the second most games in the NBA, and their team was marked by playing "small ball." Morey believed that opting for threes, layups, and free throws (in that order) represented the most efficient way to success in basketball. Today, advanced data analytics influence almost all aspects of the NBA, from evaluating and developing players to in-game decisions.

A Development of Collecting data at FIBA 3x3 Competitions

The amount of data FIBA 3x3 collects at each game is certainly not as big as what NBA collects, but FIBA 3x3 has built up their data, providing useful insights into gameplay and player and team performance.

When the World Tour started in 2012, FIBA 3x3 didn't track anything except total points scored by each team. The following year, at official competitions, FIBA 3x3 started tracking data of individual players as types of points made (ones, twos, and free throws) and players' total points. The big breakthrough came in 2017, when FIBA 3x3 implemented play-by-play commentary of games and added shots attempts, shot percentages, turnovers, blocked shots, shot efficiency, and—shortly thereafter in 2018—defensive and offensive rebounds to its comprehensive box score. With more data collected and presented, it offered a wealth of information for coaches and fans while also allowing us to compare the two basketball disciplines.

Differences in Data Collection From Traditional Basketball

FIBA 3x3 collects unique and slightly different data at games than traditional basketball leagues, so the box scores of both disciplines differentiate. Some examples are the key assist, drives, highlights, and buzzer beater, which are not tracked in traditional basketball, or else they are differently calculated. There is also a difference in calculating possessions due to contrasting formulas used by FIBA 3x3 and the NBA.

One of the shortcomings is less accurate individual player evaluation because less data have been collected. For now, it is still tough to gauge the individual players impact. Players' playing time, their plus/minus, and their shot charts are some examples of missing data in 3x3. Only so much can be gleaned from the box score; advanced data can provide so much more context, such as from where teams prefer to shoot and from where players are most efficient. Moreover, current statistics from the box chart don't always show the true value of players; players are currently valued without registering stats in the box chart—for example, number of set screens and distance covered.

Rest assured, data tracked in 3x3 will continue to progress, but in the meantime, coaches and players should rigorously analyze video to understand more. Sometimes, stats can be skewed by weather conditions or other circumstances surrounding a particular game, so everything must be examined, beyond just the current data available.

How to Properly Evaluate Performance With Stats

Per-game metrics such as points, three-pointers, and offensive rebounds define traditional basketball players and teams and are included in player bios. Take, for example the 2019–2020 NBA MVP Giannis Antetokounmpo, who had the astounding averages of 29.5 points per game, 13.6 rebounds per game, and 5.6 assists per game. These were the main stats cited when trumpeting his MVP candidacy over runner-up LeBron James. These basic stats are still the go-to because, generally, advanced data such as players' usage, block percentage, and PIE are not deeply analyzed. The "basic" data work in basketball that fans use to compare teams and players over the course of the season might be per-game metrics, though data analysts tend to look at efficiency. This is all more important in 3x3, where efficiency is the most appropriate measuring stick when comparing and analyzing different teams and players over the course of season, whereas comparison based on averages per game or season totals is certainly not appropriate and accurate enough. Does a per-game average really tell us anything in 3x3?

Why Per-Possession Metrics Are More Valuable in 3x3?

When analyzing and comparing game-related statistics of different teams over the course of a season, per possession is the single most appropriate metric to use to learn about team's efficiency. Only then can teams be properly evaluated and analyzed as "per possession" puts all teams on an equal footing no matter how many minutes or at what pace they play. Basketball games always last the same length—excepting overtime—but 3x3 can significantly vary given a winner is determined after 21 points are reached. Therefore, per-game metric is the wrong measurement for comparing teams because a team might have less stats only because their games finish quicker. A team which is extremely efficient on offense and scores 21 points fast is not worse at rebounding just because other teams average more rebounds per game. Another team might not be as efficient on offense and is unable to score 21 points in regular time. Because of that, it averages considerably longer playing time, explaining higher rebounding averages per game. So, does an average of 12 rebounds per game from one team really tell us anything when another team collects 14 rebounds per game, but the first team on average plays seven minutes per game and other nine and a half? We should really ask ourselves which team is most efficient at rebounding. This can only be done by looking at the rebounding percentage and not rebounding totals. Same goes for other game-related statistics such as turnovers or points. When we are comparing two teams, we should look at how many points per possession each team scores or allows in an effort to gauge efficiency, rather than simply comparing the per-minute or per-game statistics.

Calculating Possessions

There are specific nuances that must be kept in mind when analyzing 3x3 stats compared to those of traditional basketball. The biggest difference between data in the two disciplines is in calculating possessions. In 3x3, each opportunity to score was and still is called a possession, prescribed by FIBA 3x3's statistician manual as the number of times a team has the ball and produces one of the following possession outcomes: a one-point shot, a two-point shot, a trip to the free-throw line, or a turnover. Possessions calculated this way are called "plays" in traditional basketball, which does not extract offensive rebounds from the equation. In traditional basketball, offensive rebounds extend possession, while in 3x3, a team gains a new possession with an offensive rebound for statistical purposes. Thus, traditional basketball teams have approximately the same number of possessions during a game as their opponents, while in 3x3, teams can have larger differences. The FIBA 3x3 formula is therefore less accurate and appropriate for calculating efficiency. Any team can run the ball and shoot quickly just to score a lot of points, but that also means they give the ball back each time. Understanding this is extremely important, as efficiency is always more important than pushing up the pace.

Highly Valued 3x3 Players

The portability of a 3x3 player's skill set is critical in determining that player's value. A player who can play well on multiple 3x3 teams is more valuable than a player whose skill set fits only a few teams. For example, players who excel only in one skill, such as scoring or rebounding, are not as valuable as players with a broader skill set. Most good professional teams are already great at scoring; adding an isolation scorer will not move the needle as much as adding a pan-dimensional player. If you add XY player, who is a go-to guy for scoring points, to, for example, Princeton, they do not become a better 3x3 team. They might be worse, because the team distributes more shots to him instead of superstar Robbie Hummel or someone else. However, if you add a highly skilled 2-way versatile player to Princeton, they might become a better team. A player's defensive versatility and exceptional shooting, dribbling, rebounding, and passing skills would fit all 3x3 teams, making him extremely valuable.

In traditional basketball, player evaluation is often reduced to championship wins and averages. A player's value is also determined by what he can do on a good team rather than on a lousy team. An NBA player who improves a 45-win team to 65 wins is more valuable than a player who moves an 18-win team to 40. But when it comes to evaluating players' efficiency, every player in the NBA can be valued by the PER metric. Hollinger's player efficiency rating is a complex formula that sums up players' contributions in one number, with per-minute performance adjusted for pace. Such exact formula is still not available for 3x3 but once FIBA 3x3 starts tracking more game-related statistics at games it will be easier to properly quantify 3x3 player's performance.

COMPARISON OF GAME DATA BETWEEN 3X3 AND TRADITIONAL BASKETBALL

What are the differences between the best 3x3 teams and traditional basketball according to the stats? To answer this question, I had to tweak some of the varying metrics used by these different disciplines, but this has led to some impressive results. For the purpose of this comparison, I used data from the FIBA 3x3 World Tour and top international basketball leagues such as NBA. An explanation of the findings is presented in the following sections, and readers can find tables with accurate and precise data in tables in this chapter. The purpose of the comparison was to find which basketball discipline has more efficient teams when executing certain skills and what their habits and characteristics are merely by looking at the game-related stats. For the sake of simplicity, I'll use 3x3's scoring terms to refer to both disciplines: a one-point shot and a two-point shot in 3x3 are a two-point shot and a three-point shot in traditional basketball respectively.

Shooting

Shooting efficiently is important in both disciplines, but every shot in 3x3 has a higher stake than in traditional basketball since the game only lasts for 10 minutes or to 21 points. Let's first look at the shot distribution in each discipline. The most frequently attempted shot in both disciplines is the one-pointer (inside the arc), representing about 50% of total shots. However, the two-point shot (outside the arc) is more prevalent in 3x3, amounting to about 40% of shots, with fewer free throws. In traditional basketball, there is more balance between attempted free throws (20%) and attempted two-point shots (30%).

Analyzing the shot distribution between 3x3 and traditional basketball competitions over a few seasons reveals the pattern that 3×3 players have a higher frequency of two-point shots attempted and a lower frequency of free throw shots attempted while having higher or roughly the same frequency of one-point shots attempted. The 2019 3x3 WT season had a 9.2 p.p. lower free-throw frequency, for 0.9 p.p. higher one-point frequency and 8.3 p.p. higher two-point frequency, compared to the 2019–2020 NBA season.

We must also point out the shooting percentage difference. Generally, 3x3's shooting percentage compared to basketball is lower for two-point shots and free throws but higher for one-point shots. The 2019 3x3 WT season compared to the 2019–2020 NBA season had an 8.9 p.p. lower shooting percentage from outside the arc and a 12.6 p.p. lower free-throw shooting percentage. Overall, total shooting percentage in 3x3 is lower (4.6 p.p. lower in the 2020 WT season compared to the 2019–2020 NBA season), but thus can be attributed to the pressures of outdoor conditions, more physical contact, and a shorter shot clock, which can contribute to rushed and unbalanced shots.

The Value of Shots From Outside the Arc

The NBA transformed basketball by implementing the three-point line for the 1979–1980 season. It took decades for teams to value the shot and specifically strategize for it, but now, decades later, the three-pointer has completely changed every facet of the game. Savvy analysts like Morey, understood the mathematical advantage of three-pointers and started building their teams around specialist shooters. In 2012, before some of the more sophisticated data was available to teams, NBA teams only took 18.4 three-pointers per game. This almost doubled by 2019–2020, when an average of 34.1 were attempted. Prior to 2015–2016, no NBA player had ever made 300 three-pointers in a single season, but that season's MVP Steph Curry—the best three-point shooter in NBA history—sank an incredible 402. During the 2018–2019 regular season, NBA players made 27,955 three-point shots—more than in the entire decade of the 1980s (23,871), when the three-pointer was still not valued, and teams believed dominating inside was the necessary formula for success. Surprisingly, during the 2019–2020 season, Morey's Rockets doubled down on their "small ball" style and attempted more threes than twos over the course of the season. The trend is clear, and it seems that teams in the modern NBA have realized the importance of threes, which are 50% more valuable than twos. But in 3x3, there is even more value in shots from outside the arc, with two-pointers being 100% more valuable than one-point shots from inside the arc. It means there is even more of an outside game in 3x3, and its why sharpshooters are worth their weight in gold.

Free Throws

3x3 players shoot free throws during the game less frequently compared to traditional basketball players because the foul threshold is different. In 3x3, teams are in the bonus—where free throws are awarded—after the sixth foul, whereas in some traditional basketball leagues, the threshold is four fouls. In the NBA, each team is limited to four team fouls in a quarter, or two fouls in the last two minutes of a quarter. 3x3 also allows more physical contact, and referees are more likely to be lenient with their whistles. Especially in the NBA, fouls are called regularly, with star players often receiving the benefit of the doubt if even receiving the slightest contact from defenders. In the 2020 3x3 WT season, the free-throw rate, which tells us the team's ability to get to the free-throw line, was 5.9 p.p. lower than in the 2019–2020 NBA season.

One-Point Shots

The frequency of one-pointers (shots from inside the arc) is about the same in traditional basketball and 3x3, but there is a higher percentage in the latter because a common tactic is to allow uncontested layups to prevent two-pointers being attempted. The 2020 FIBA 3x3 WT teams had a one-point shot percentage 6.1 p.p. higher than teams in the 2019–2020 NBA regular season. I can say from experience playing and watching 3x3 games (not based on stats) that midrange shots in 3x3 are not common. This is similar to traditional basketball, in which midrange shots have been discouraged for the last few years in the NBA because analysts consider them inefficient.

Effective Field Goal Percentage

The effective field goal percentage tells us who is scoring more effectively from the field. It is nearly the same in both disciplines, with the 2020 FIBA 3x3 WT 3.6 p.p. higher than the 2019–2020 NBA regular season. However, the best 3x3 teams have a much higher effective field goal percentage than top basketball teams. Novi Sad had an effective field goal percentage 6.86 p.p. higher than the Los Angeles Lakers, who were the NBA champions in the 2019–2020 season. In traditional basketball, effective field goal percentage represents one of the most important stats. For example, in the 2018–2019 NBA season, the Golden State Warriors had the highest average, and the Toronto Raptors had the fourth highest average in the league, and they both played in the NBA final that year.

Effective field goal percentage in 3x3 adjusts the percentage of one-point and two-point shots to accommodate the fact that a two-point shot is worth 100% more than a one-point shot. That value justifies why 3x3 teams shoot more two-pointers than basketball teams shoot threes, although the trend of shooting threes has been rapidly increasing in the NBA.

Shooting Comparison Between Men's and Women's Categories

Regarding shooting distribution, there is a much higher frequency of one-point shots attempted in women's professional 3x3, but there are fewer two-pointers and free throws attempted compared to the men's teams. The 2019 3x3 Women's Series had a 2.1 p.p. lower free-throw frequency, 5.7 p.p. lower two-point frequency and a 7.8 p.p. higher one-point frequency compared to the 2019 3x3 World Tour season. Thus, one-point shots in women's 3x3 are by far the most frequent (averages for the 2019 Women's Series are a 9.3% free-throw frequency, a 57.6% one-point frequency, and a 33.1% two-point frequency). The shooting efficiency is not at the same level as males (the 2019 Women's Series total shot percentage was for 6.8 p.p. lower than on the 2020 3x3 World Tour).

Now let's look at the comparison between women's 3x3 competition and traditional basketball competition. When comparing shooting efficiency in the 2019 Women's Series season with traditional basketball's 2019 FIBA Women's World Cup, the total shot percentage is for 6.8 p.p. lower, the two-point shot percentage is 6.5 p.p. lower, and the one-point shot percentage is 1.6 p.p. higher. When comparing shooting distribution between these two women's competitions women in 3x3 attempt free throws less frequently but more one-pointers and two-pointers. The free-throw frequency is lower by 12.8 p.p., the one-point frequency is higher by 4.3 p.p., and the two-point frequency is higher by 8.5 p.p. in the 3x3 Women's Series.

Table 28: Team season averages in international traditional basketball leagues

Season	FT Freq %	2-pt Freq %	3-pt Freq %	FT %	2-pt %	3-pt %	Total shot %	EFG%
FIBA WC 2019	22.3	48.3	29.4	74.9	50.5	34	50.9	NA
FIBA EC 2017	24.3	46.9	28.8	76.1	51.3	34.5	52.5	NA
NBA 2019–2020	20.6	48.9	30.5	77.3	52.4	34.1	52.5	52.9
LAL 2019–2020	21.6	50.3	28.1	72.9	55.2	34.9	53.3	54.2
MIA 2019–2020	23.0	44.7	32.3	78.3	53.2	37.9	54.0	54.7
Liga ACB 2019–2020	22.6	46	31.4	75.2	52.4	35.4	52.3	52.7

(continued)

3X3 BASKETBALL ★

(Tab. 28, continued)

Season	FT Freq %	2-pt Freq %	3-pt Freq %	FT %	2-pt %	3-pt %	Total shot %	EFG%
RM ACB 2019–2020	23.6	42.9	33.5	78.1	53.7	38.9	54.5	55.7
LNB Pro A 2019–2020	24.1	47.7	28.2	75.1	53.6	37.7	54.3	54.7
NBL 2019–2020	22	47.8	30.2	75.8	52.5	36.0	52.7	53.1
CBA 2019–2020	24.5	49.2	26.3	74.2	52.9	35.2	53.5	52.9
NBA 2018–2019	20.6	50.9	28.5	76.6	52.0	35.5	52.3	52.4

Table 29: FIBA 3x3 World Tour season averages

Season	FT Freq %	1-pt Freq %	2-pt Freq %	FT %	1-pt %	2-pt %	Total shot %
WT 2020 (all teams)	12.5	48.3	39.2	69.8	58.5	27.0	47.6
WT 2019 (all teams)	11.4	49.8	38.8	64.7	55.7	25.2	44.9
WT 2019 (top 10)	12.3	48.4	39.3	65.9	58.9	27.1	47.3
WT 2018 (top 10	11.3	48.4	40.3	59.6	59.5	25.3	45.7
WT 2018 (all teams)	10.8	49	40.2	59.7	56	24.6	43.8
WT 2017 (top 10)	10.7	46.1	43.2	61.9	58.8	27.0	45.4
WT 2017 (all teams)	9.8	48.6	41.6	61.3	53.5	25.4	42.6

Table 30: FIBA 3x3 World Tour and its team season averages

Season	FT %	1-pt %	2-pt %	EFG %
WT 2020	69.8	58.5	27.0	56.5
WT 2019	64.7	55.7	25.2	53.4
Novi Sad 2019	72.0	64.5	28.2	61.0
Princeton 2019	74.4	56.6	30.9	59.1
Liman 2019	63.7	65.2	24.8	57.9
Riga 2019	57.8	57.5	28.1	56.8
WT 2018	59.7	55.8	24.6	52.9
Novi Sad 2018	72	64	29.6	62.2
Liman 2018	60.6	67	26.0	60.1
Riga 2018	62.5	58	21.6	50.6
Princeton 2018	54.5	52.3	27.8	53.9
WT 2017	61.3	53.5	25.4	52.2

Table 31: NBA free-throw rate percentage season averages

Season	FTR %
NBA 2019–2020	20.1
NBA 2018–2019	19.8
NBA 2010–2011	22.9

Table 32: FIBA 3x3 WT free-throw rate percentage season averages

Season	FTR %
WT 2020	14.2
WT 2019	12.8
WT 2018	12.1

Table 33: Women's international traditional basketball competition averages

Season	FT Freq %	2-pt Freq %	3-pt Freq %	FT %	1-pt %	2-pt %	Total shot %
FIBA WC 2019	22.1	53.3	24.6	72	45.1	30.1	47.4
FIBA EC 2018	21.3	56	22.7	70.6	45.5	32.2	47.9

Table 34: FIBA 3x3 Women's Series season averages

Season	FT Freq %	1-pt Freq %	2-pt Freq %	FT %	1-pt %	2-pt %	Total shot %
WS 2019 (all)	9.3	57.6	33.1	65.1	46.7	23.6	40.8
WS 2019 (top 10)	10.5	55.1	34.4	66.6	53.6	23.8	44.7

Pace

3x3 is played at more than 1.5 times the pace of traditional basketball. This is due to the 12-second shot clock and playing on only one basket. Pace tells us how many possessions a team uses per 48 minutes in NBA or 10 minutes in 3x3. If we adjust the FIBA 3x3 possession formula, subtract offensive rebounds from the equation, and adjust 2020 World Tour games to 48 minutes, like in the NBA, teams would have approximately 160.2 possessions per game—compared to 100.3 possession per game in the 2019–2020 NBA season. Because 3x3 teams more frequently "extend possessions" with offensive rebounds then NBA counterparts, it is also interesting to see how many field goals a 3x3 team would attempt in a 48-minute game. By data from the 2020 World Tour season, 3x3 teams would attempt 65.7% more field goals in a 48-minute game than NBA teams did in the 2019–2020 season.

3X3 BASKETBALL ★

Table 35: Pace averages per game in the NBA

Season	Pace
NBA 2019–2020	100.3
LAL 2019–2020	100.9
MIA 2019–2020	98.3
NBA 2018–2019	100
GS 2018–2019	101.7
NBA 2017–2018	97.3
NBA 2010–2011	92.1

Table 36: FIBA 3x3 World Tour pace averages for a 48-minute game
(with possession formula adjusted to NBA's possession formula)

Season	Pace/48 min
WT 2020	160.2
WT 2019	156.7
WT 2018	156.06

Table 37: NBA field goal attempts per game

Season	FGA
NBA 2019–2020	88.8
NBA 2018–2019	89.2

Table 38: FIBA 3x3 World Tour field goal attempts per 48 minutes

Season	FGA/48 min
WT 2020	147.1
WT 2019	145.1
WT 2018	144.9

Offensive and Defensive Efficiency Rating

Offensive and defensive ratings—used by both disciplines—give an evaluation of efficiency and are adjusted for pace, calculating points scored and allowed on a per-possession basis. In other words, they measure how many points a team scores or allows per 100 possessions. The greater the offensive rating, the greater efficiency a player or a team has at scoring points during possessions.

When scoring and possessions are adjusted accordingly, traditional basketball teams tend to be more efficient at scoring points per possession than their 3x3 counterparts. In theory, that means 3x3 basketball teams have a higher defensive rating than their traditional basketball counterparts to the same degree that they have a lower offensive rating.

Offensive efficiency in basketball is more balanced among all teams, while in 3x3 there is a greater difference between winning and losing teams. When scoring is adjusted, NBA teams in the 2019–2020 season had a 12.74 p.p. higher offensive rating on average than 3x3 teams in the 2019 FIBA 3x3 WT. However, the best 3x3 teams, such as Liman, Riga, and Novi Sad, are more efficient offensively than best NBA teams. In the 2019 season, if scoring is adjusted to match traditional basketball, Novi Sad had a 7.04 p.p. higher offensive rating than the NBA champions, the Los Angeles Lakers, during their 2019–2020 NBA regular season. It is clear that the discrimination between good and bad teams in 3x3 is much greater than in traditional basketball.

Table 39: NBA offensive rating averages by games

Season	OFF rat
NBA 2019–2020	111.4
LAL 2019–2020	112
MIA 2019–2020	112.5
NBA 2018–2019	110.4
GS 2018–2019	115.7
LAL 2018–2019	107.9
NBA 2017–2018	109.2
NBA 2010–2011	107.3
NBA 2000–2001	103

Table 40: FIBA 3x3 WT offensive rating averages by game (scoring and possession formula adjusted to traditional basketball rules)

Season	OFF rat
WT 2020	101.8
WT 2019	98.66
Novi Sad 2019	119.04
Princeton 2019	114.69
Riga 2019	121.36
WT 2018	96.7
Novi Sad 2018	124
Liman 2018	119.8

Rebounding

The rebounding percentage tells us exactly how efficient one team is at rebounding. The offensive rebound percentage measures the available offensive rebounds that a team recovers. The offensive rebound percentage is higher and the defensive rebound percentage lower in 3x3 than in traditional basketball.

In the 2020 3x3 World Tour season, teams had an average offensive rebound percentage 11.4 p.p. higher than teams in the 2019–2020 NBA season. This is a big difference, illustrating that 3x3 teams are more effective after offensive rebounds but less effective after defensive rebounds than in traditional basketball. The reason for this dissimilarity is in the fact that 3x3 only has one basket, so all offensive players can theoretically crash the offensive board. In traditional basketball, some offensive players need to be ready to push back to the other basket in case they need to thwart fast breaks from their opponents.

Table 41: Rebound percentages in traditional basketball leagues

Season	OFF REB %	DEF REB %
NBA 2019–2020	22.5	77.5
LAL 2019–2020	24.5	78.8
MIA 2019–2020	20.3	79.5
Liga ACB 2019–2020	29.2	70.8
RM ACB 2019–2020	28.1	71.8
LNB Pro A 2019–2020	27.3	72.7
NBL 2019–2020	28.6	71.4
CBA 2019–2020	28	72
NBA 2018–2019	22.9	77.1
NBA MIL 2018–2019	20.8	80.3
NBA TOR 2018–2019	21.9	77.1

Table 42: FIBA 3x3 World Tour rebounding percentages

Season	OFF REB %	DEF REB %
WT 2020	33.9	66.1
WT 2019	33.3	66.7
Novi Sad 2019	29.1	68.4
Princeton 2019	27.8	69.4
Riga 2019	41.1	71.8
WT 2018	34.6	65.4
Novi Sad 2018	33.73	65.6

Turnovers

Turnover percentage, which shows as an estimate of turnovers per 100 possessions, is higher by a small margin in 3x3. The 2020 World Tour season had a 1.8 p.p. higher turnover percentage than the NBA 2019–2020 season. This underlines the importance of players properly caring for the ball in both disciplines. The 3x3 turnover percentage is higher due to the shorter shot clock, the fast transitions and the higher degree of physical contact allowed on defense. For all these reasons, the best 3x3 teams avoid any unnecessary dribbling.

Table 43: NBA turnover percentages

Season	TO %
NBA 2019–2020	12.8
LAL 2019–2020	13.3
MIA 2019–2020	13.5
NBA 2018–2019	12.4

Table 44: FIBA 3x3 World Tour turnover percentages

Season	TO %
WT 2020	14.6
WT 2019	14.4
WT 2018	15.4

STATISTICAL ANALYSIS OF WORLD TOUR SEASONS

Like all sports in their beginning years, 3x3 has evolved markedly over the last decade. With added knowledge and data, coaches and players better understand 3x3, and the game has adjusted accordingly. Let's look at how the data has helped to shape 3x3.

Current professional 3x3 teams:

★ tend to win games faster, as they score 21 points more quickly (WBL %).

★ score more points per game on average (PTS).

★ shoot more efficiently, as they have higher shooting percentages (Total Shot %; EFG %).

★ attempt and make free throws more frequently (FT) and score more of their points from free throws (%PTS FT).

★ shoot two-pointers more efficiently since the beginning of the World Tour but score fewer of their points from two-pointers (%PTS 2-pt). It seems the right balance has been found between inside and outside scoring.

★ commit and receive more fouls due to more aggressive and sophisticated defense (TF; TFA).

★ substitute at a higher rate due to the game's increased intensity.

Table 45: Averages per game for FIBA 3x3 World Tour, part 1

World Tour	PTS	WBL %	FTM	FTA	FT %	FT Freq %	% PTS FT	1-ptm	1-pta	1-pt %	1-pt Freq %	% PTS 1-pt
2020 (all teams)	17.7	34.6	2.65	3.79	69.8	12.5	15.0	8.62	14.7	58.5	48.3	48.6
2019 (all teams)	17.0	30	2.3	3.6	64.7	11.4	13.5	8.6	15.5	55.7	50	50.7
2019 (top 10)	18.3	44	2.6	3.9	65.9	12.3	14	9.0	15.3	58.9	48.4	49.3
2018 (all teams)	16.9	30.5	2.0	3.41	59.7	10.8	12.7	8.6	15.5	55.8	49.0	50.9
2018 (top 10)	18.0	40.7	2.2	3.7	59.6	11.3	12.2	9.3	15.7	59.5	48.4	51.6
2017 (all teams)	16.6	28	1.9	3.1	61.3	9.8	11.3	8.1	15.2	53.5	48.6	48.9
2017 (top 10)	18.1	40.3	2.1	3.4	61.9	10.7	11.6	8.6	14.6	58.8	46.1	47.5

Table 46: Averages per game for FIBA 3x3 World Tour, part 2

World Tour	2-ptm	2-pta	2-pt %	2-pt Freq %	%PTS 2-pt	Total shot %	TO	OFF REB	OFF REB %	DEF REB	DEF REB %	TOT REB	TF	TFA
2020 (all teams)	3.2	11.9	27.02	39.2	36.4	47.6	5	5.12	33.9	10.0	66.1	15.1	7.0	7.0
2019 (all teams)	3.05	12.1	25.2	39	35.8	44.9	5.21	5.4	33.3	10.9	66.7	16.3	6.8	6.8
2019 (top 10)	3.37	12.44	27.1	39.3	36.7	47.3	4.9	5.6	32.7	11.4	67.3	17.0	6.7	7.0
2018 (all teams)	3.12	12.7	24.6	40.2	36.9	43.7	5.6	5.8	34.6	11.0	65.4	16.9	6.4	6.4
2018 (top 10)	3.3	13.1	25.3	40.2	36.6	45.7	5.42	6.4	36.3	11.3	63.7	17.7	6.3	6.8
2017 (all teams)	3.3	13.0	25.4	41.6	39.7	42.6	4.8						5.7	5.7
2017 (top 10)	3.7	13.7	27.1	43.2	40.9	45.4	3.8						5.9	6.0

Table 47: Team averages per game at FIBA 3x3 World Tour Finals

WT Finals	PTS	2-ptm	WBL %
2013	15.1	2.2	24
2015	16.4	2.66	42.1
2017	16.6	2.74	52.6
2019	17.6	3	57.9

Substitutions

3x3 teams should substitute at such a rate that it doesn't affect their performance and rhythm. The amount of time spent on the bench and the number of substitutions in a game depends on the number of dead-ball situations. A trend in recent years has been that teams substitute more frequently than they used to. This is to ensure their intensity level remains consistent throughout the game; substituting at a higher rate with shorter bench times has proven to be more beneficial than sitting for longer stretches.

An analysis of the 2014 and 2019 World Tour Finals shows a huge difference in substitutions, with a 36 p.p. higher substitution rate in the 2019 Final. 3x3 Novi Sad played in both events, and their substitution rate was 24.9 p.p. higher in 2019 than in 2014. The analysis also showed that teams tend to substitute at different rates during the game based on different factors. There is a lower rate in the first minute of a game because players are not yet tired enough to need substitution. There is also a lower rate in the last minute; the reasons for this are:

★ A one-sided game is effectively decided, and substitutions are of no use anymore.

★ Teams want to use their three best players at the end of the game, and they often will set this up earlier since it is unknown when a dead-ball situation will occur.

★ Players are confident they have the energy to finish the game or believe they can contribute more than the substitute and do not want to be substituted.

Table 48: Substitution rate at the 2014 and 2019 FIBA 3x3 World Tour Finals
(data collection and its analysis by the author; semi-final and final games)

WT Final	SR for whole game	SR for first minute	SR between first and last minute	SR for last minute	SR after time-outs
2019 (all teams)	58.2	45.8	66.2	22.7	75.0
2014 (all teams)	22.2	0	30.4	23.1	40
2019 (Novi Sad)	61.9	30	73.3	37.5	83.3
2014 Novi Sad)	37	0	40.5	42.9	66.7

Close Games in World Tour History

Due to the low scoring and tight time frame, 3x3 is more prone to close games than traditional basketball, which usually lasts 40 or 48 minutes. Of all FIBA 3x3 World Tour games from 2012 to 2020, 26.34% have finished with a two- or one-point differential, meaning the slightest circumstance can swing a 3x3 game. Bear in mind that a two-point differential can be compensated in only one possession!

Table 49: Percentage of games with a differential of two or fewer points at the FIBA 3x3 World Tour (data collection and analysis by author)

World Tour	Games with a difference of 2 PTS or fewer	All games	% of games with a difference of 2 PTS or fewer
2020	25	94	26.6
2019	50	228	21.9
2018	50	190	26.3
2017	37	152	24.3
2016	27	152	17.8
2015	40	133	30
2014	36	133	27.1
2013	43	150	28.7
2012	76	226	33.6
2012–2020	384	1458	26.34

Performance of High-Ranked Teams on the World Tour

In traditional basketball, earning a top seed is a huge advantage. Higher-seeded teams tend to be more successful, and they rarely face upsets in the first round of elimination phases. In the NCAA Division 1, before the University of Maryland upset the Virginia Cavaliers in the 2018 season, 16-seeded teams were 0-132 against 1-seeds. In the NBA, since the league expanded the playoffs to 16 teams in the 1983–1984 season, No. 1 seeds in the East and West combined have won 69 of the 74 first-round series against No. 8 seeds prior to the 2021 season.

Is a top seed a huge advantage also in 3x3? In all FIBA 3x3 official competitions and prior to 3x3 tournaments, teams are seeded based on their world ranking. So how successful are higher-ranked teams when playing lower-ranked teams at the

World Tour? In order to understand that, we have to look at a comparison of all games from the 2015 to the 2020 World Tour season. During that time period, higher-ranked teams have won 72.4% of 949 games.

Table 50: Win percentages of higher-ranked teams on the FIBA 3x3 World Tour (data collection and analysis by author)

World Tour	Wins	Games	Win %
2020	65	94	69.2
2019	170	228	74.6
2018	140	190	77.9
2017	115	152	75.0
2016	101	152	66.4
2015	96	133	72.2
2015–2020	687	949	72.4

Dividing a 3x3 Game Into Two Halves of the Same Playing Time

It is important to understand how a 3x3 game unwinds. If we divide it into two imaginary halves of equal playing time, how would statistics differ between the two halves? After analyzing all the games of the 2018 and 2019 World Tour Finals, I concluded that the second half of a game has significantly more scoring. Teams in the 2019 World Tour Final scored more points in the second half than in the first by 10.08 p.p., while teams in the 2018 World Tour Final scored more points in the second half by 13.35 p.p. Furthermore, 3x3 teams made more shots of all kinds in the second half but committed fewer fouls. The biggest difference is in made free throws, as the number of free throws increase throughout the game as teams get into bonus situations after opponents hit the foul threshold, usually late in the game. Teams in the 2019 World Tour Final made more free throws in the second half by 25.72 p.p., and in the 2018 World Tour Final by 42.6 p.p.

There is significantly more scoring in the second half of a game due to:

★ defensive teams hitting the foul threshold, which gives the opposition free throws.

★ defense becoming less aggressive because teams try to avoid making fouls and giving the opposition free throws once they have reached foul bonus.

★ the onset of fatigue leading to a deterioration of defense.

Table 51: Ratio between averages of "one half" with averages of whole game in 19 games at the 2019 FIBA 3x3 World Tour Final. Expressed in percentages (data collection and analysis by author)

2019 WT Final	1st half	2nd half	Whole game
PTS	44.9	55.1	100
FTM	45.0	55.0	100
1-ptm	47.3	52.7	100
2-ptm	37.1	62.9	100
TF	60.6	39.4	100
Playing time	4:38	4:38	9:16

Table 52: Ratio between averages of "one half" with averages of whole game in 19 games at the 2018 FIBA 3x3 World Tour Final. Expressed in percentages (data collection and analysis by author)

2018 Final WT	1st half	2nd half	Whole game
PTS	43.3	56.7	100
FTM	42.2	57.8	100
1-ptm	47.5	52.4	100
2-ptm	28.7	71.3	100
TF	52.7	47.3	100
Playing time	4:48	4:48	9:36

Game-Related Statistics and Results

Discriminatory analysis between winning and losing teams was made in an attempt to present how a single game-related factor affects results. For the purpose of the analysis, all games from the 2020 and 2019 World Tour seasons were combined in one statistical base (n=322) and later analyzed. Statistical factors possession (sc = 0.441) and defensive rebounding (sc = 0.335) had the highest discriminatory value from all analyzed factors. For even clearer understanding of how factors impact the outcome, all games were further divided to balanced—a point differential between a winning and losing team is three points or less—and unbalanced—a point differential is four points or more. Values of winning and losing teams are presented and can be easily compared and comprehended.

Table 53: Averages of the game-related statistical factors of all games
(mean ± s, n=322, analysis by author)

Game-related statistics	Winning teams	Losing teams
Points	19.98 ± 2.13	14.68 ± 3.22
1-ptm	9.47 ± 2.74	7.95 ± 2.60
1-ptm %	61.75 ± 13.42	53.22 ± 14.4
2-ptm	3.69 ± 1.79	2.42 ± 1.51
2-pt %	31.10 ± 15.06	20.83 ± 12.59
FTM	3.14 ± 2.27	1.89 ± 1.56
FT %	67.13 ± 30.79	58.69 ± 35.74
OFF REB	5.60 ± 2.84	5.32 ± 2.79
DEF REB	11.64 ± 3.56	9.75 ± 3.66
REB	17.23 ± 4.92	15.06 ± 4.88
TO	4.66 ± 2.22	5.65 ± 2.52
FOULS	6.45 ± 1.98	7.42 ± 2.13
KAS	3.39 ± 1.95	2.21 ± 1.52
BS	1.04 ± 1.13	0.91 ± 0.98

3X3 BASKETBALL ★

Table 54: Averages of the game-related statistical factors of balanced games
(mean ± s, analysis by author)

Game-related statistics	Winning teams	Losing teams
Points	18.78 ± 2.60	16.80 ± 2.70
1-ptm	9.22 ± 2.58	8.93 ± 2.54
1-ptm %	57.55 ± 12.29	54.39 ± 13.11
2-ptm	3.35 ± 1.75	2.80 ± 1.58
2-pt %	27.03 ± 15.10	23.13 ± 12.99
FTM	2.84 ± 2.10	2.26 ± 1.81
FT %	62.74 ± 31.22	60.74 ± 33.50
OFF REB	5.66 ± 2.72	5.73 ± 2.79
DEF REB	11.67 ± 3.30	11.51 ± 3.77
REB	17.33 ± 4.19	17.25 ± 4.68
TO	5.23± 2.25	5.84 ± 2.69
FOULS	6.99 ± 1.66	7.58± 1.67
KAS	2.83 ± 1.58	2.64 ± 1.53
BS	1.12 ± 1.14	0.98 ± 0.99

Table 55: Averages of the game-related statistical factors of unbalanced
games (mean ± s, analysis by author)

Game-related statistics	Winning teams	Losing teams
Points	20.67 ± 1.39	13.38 ± 2.81
1-ptm	9.60 ± 2.82	7.35 ± 2.46
1-ptm %	64.17 ± 13.47	52.49 ± 15.17
2-ptm	3.88 ± 1.78	2.18 ± 1.42
2-ptm %	33.44 ± 14.57	19.41 ± 12.14
FTM	3.31 ± 2.36	1.65 ± 1.33
FT %	69.65 ± 30.33	57.42 ± 37.08
OFF REB	5.55 ± 2.91	5.06 ± 2.76
DEF REB	11.62 ± 3.71	8.65 ± 3.12
REB	17.17 ± 5.31	13.71 ± 4.50
TO	4.33 ± 2.13	5.53 ± 2.41
FOULS	6.14 ± 2.08	7.32 ± 2.36
KAS	3.71 ± 2.06	1.94 ± 1.44
BS	0.99 ± 1.13	0.87 ± 0.97

CHAPTER 8
3X3 TACTICS

A THEORETICAL EXPLANATION OF 3X3 TACTICS

Good 3x3 play involves the rational selection of individual, two-man, and team tactics to achieve the best possible in-game results. Teams need to execute their tactics in such a way as to optimize team play based on strengths and to exploit as much of the team's potential as possible, especially of those players who are most effective.[29]

In a sign of the growing professionalism of 3x3, tactics are playing an increasingly important role. Modern 3x3 team tactics are becoming more complex, though they are still not at the level of traditional basketball given the smaller number of players on the court and the newness of the sport.

Tactics in 3x3 can be broken down by whether a team is on offense or on defense and subsequently by game phase: check-ball phase, direct transition phase, and indirect transition phase. These tactics are similar to those of traditional basketball, but there are different nuances in 3x3 due to the differing style of the games and rules.

3x3 players also need to think about individual tactics, two-player tactics, and team tactics.

★ **Individual tactics** are employed by an individual player without the direct assistance of a teammate. When players go one-on-one with an opponent, it requires tactical intelligence and creativity.

★ **Two-player tactics** are those in which two players on one team participate. The players can execute them as a part of vision for team tactics. Two-player tactics are developed in two-on-two games, which often help create chemistry between a team's two best players. Many important set plays are derived from the two-man game, such as the pick and roll and pick and pop.

★ **Team tactics** include the cooperation and participation of all three players on the team. Team tactics require all the players to unite for a specific goal simultaneously.[29]

Setting and Adjusting Tactics

Having set principles and predetermined tactical combinations is necessary. If gameplay is left totally to instinct, things can get chaotic under pressure. Coach can set tactics before the start of the event; however, during the games, the players need to be able to adjust and change tactics properly. Coaches need to find the balance between structure and letting their players perform on intuition. There should be flexibility to revert to one or the other during games. Therefore, team tactics should be prearranged and rehearsed, but athletes should be able to adapt them during a game. This requires quick and efficient problem-solving as well as good decision-making skills.

FUNDAMENTAL TEAM TACTICS

Team Tactics on Offense

Team tactics on offense require the cooperation and the desire of offensive players without the ball to help the offensive player with the ball play successfully.[27] The best teams share the ball and have dynamic play, with offensive actions and movements that ensure multiple attack options. For that reason and to have the best chance to win the game, a team's playbook should contain numerous transition and check-ball offensive plays, which include all three players—or, if that is not possible, at least two players. One-on-one isolation plays should be used as a last resort, because they demand a lot of energy from an individual player and stop team movement, among other disadvantages.

Compared to traditional basketball, the 3x3 playbook doesn't involve zone offensive plays or inbound offensive plays. Furthermore, basketball teams use far more schematic and organized offensive team tactics compared to teams in 3x3, where an offensive player often trades on a healthy dose of creativity, instinct, and improvisation.

Rules for a Successful 3x3 Offense

1. *Commit to excellence!* Give your best!

2. *Communicate.* Communicate E.L.C. (early, loud, and continually).

3. *Show energy.* Teams that move the ball have great energy.

4. *Move and be active.* Every player on a team needs to move and be active all the time. Moving players need to be aware of spacing.

5. *Read and react.* Read the defense and react to it with well-tuned intuition and instincts.

6. *Be aggressive; be an offensive threat.* Be aggressive toward the basket, look to score or help a teammate score.

7. **Balance.** Attack the rim, don't just shoot two-pointers. Be dangerous from inside and outside.

8. **Concentrate.** Concentrate on every play. The game lasts just 10 minutes. Mental focus is key.

9. **Take care of the ball.** Minimize turnovers.

10. **Maintain court awareness.** Know where the ball and players are on the court. Always be conscious of the 12-second shot clock.

11. **Take second chances.** Crash the offensive glass or set good initial defensive position.

12. **Conquer the space.** Since there is a lot more space to conquer in 3x3 compared to basketball, this element is extremely important. Conquer the space, out-position the defender, and get open using physicality, speed, or change of direction.

13. **Work as a team.** Sharing the ball and teamwork are crucial for success.

Offensive Tactics in the Transition Phase

After gaining possession of the ball, teams in transition offense aim to score in a matter of seconds through an offensive play called quick-hitter, but if they can't, then they try to attack against yet unestablished defenses through an offensive play called early offense. If that fails, then they attack against set defenses with either schematic, organized, or improvised plays.

The Quick-Hitter

Quick-hitter is an offensive play in which the offensive team quickly creates a scoring opportunity to try to attack and take advantage of a defense that is not yet set. Most often, the offensive team makes only one quick pass to clear the ball and then immediately takes a shot. The goal is to move into scoring position as quickly as possible, so that the defensive team doesn't have time to set up. This play is also efficient in indirect transition offense when a player from a non-scoring team quickly picks up the ball after receiving a basket and then clears the ball with a pass outside the two-point arc, and a teammate who receives the pass immediately shoots or passes the ball back inside for uncontested layup (clear the ball and seal). A well-executed quick-hitter is a feature of top professional 3x3 teams, as it leads to easy baskets in a matter of seconds after the transition on offense, fueling confidence and gaining a psychological stranglehold on opponents. Teams can execute the quick-hitter after a steal, a defensive rebound, or even a made basket.

Pass and Seal

This is an efficient way of scoring an easy and quick basket. The offensive player who has just transitioned from defense to offense and has acquired possession of the ball under the basket (through a defensive rebound or by picking up the ball after a made basket) should quickly clear the ball with a pass and seal a defensive player under the basket. This will catch the defense by surprise and enable an easy finish. So, how exactly do you execute this? First, an offensive player under the basket who has just acquired possession of the ball should quickly and accurately pass the ball to a teammate outside the two-point arc. He then immediately ducks in, seals a defensive player under the basket, reaches out a hand, and signals to a teammate that he wants the ball back. If a teammate can quickly free up from his defender, receive the pass, and then quickly and accurately pass the ball back inside, an offensive player under the basket can score an easy layup.

Early Offense

Early offense is an offensive play in which after failing to take advantage of a quick hitter, an offensive team continues to attack against not set or outnumbered defensive players in a bid to exploit late defensive closeouts or mismatches. Like with the quick-hitters, the offensive team forces the defense to react rather than act.

The Set Offense: A Tactic in the Transition and Check-ball Phases

An offensive set play can occur both in the check-ball and transition phases. It is an offensive play against an established defense and is necessary in the transition phase when teams don't take advantage of a quick-hitter or early offense. All three players take part in the offensive set play with a coordinated spatial and temporal movement. An offensive set play can be schematic, improvised, organized, or a combination of these.

Schematic Plays

Schematic plays require players to operate strictly within a particular system regardless of the defense's placement. Schematic plays are designed to get specific players the ball in certain areas of the floor. Unlike improvised plays, they clearly specify each player's actions and tasks, the entries of the play, and how to finish the play. Schematic plays are extremely rare in transition offense due to the short shot clock; however, this method is frequently used in check-ball offenses.

Improvised Plays

Improvised plays are based on extremely fast individual solutions: players "read and react" without a predetermined tactical plan. This method is especially evident in players able to solve situations spontaneously and instinctively. It is impossible to successfully implement it without a high basketball IQ. Improvised plays are especially common for amateur teams, who tend to play a more unorganized game compared to the professional ranks. Moreover, this method can be prone to misunderstandings between players, leading to bad plays if players do not have a lot of experience playing together.

Organized Plays (Principles-Based Plays)

Organized, or principles-based, plays are when an offensive team follows certain principles and has sensibly arranged players on the court to achieve a preferred offense, but it also leaves room for player creativity and decision-making. This is the method most commonly used by professional 3x3 teams. Teams determine their principles pre-game but often need to use their instincts to overcome problems that arise in games. Structurally, this method is somewhere between an improvised and schematic play.

The positive features of principles-based plays are:

★ Principles-based plays assign specific roles and tasks to individual players in the offense, which increases their self-confidence and determination.

★ Players know in advance what they can and can't do and what they need to do in the play.

★ Principles-based plays allow offensive players to systematically attack the disadvantages of defensive players.

★ Principles-based plays determine a sensible selection of shots and passes and punish opponents' errors on defense.

★ Principles-based plays allow coordinated movement of offensive players, leading to open shots and beneficial mismatches.

★ Principles-based plays leave more creativity and in-game decision-making to players than schematic plays.

Offensive Tactics in Check-ball Phase

Teams in a check-ball offense don't use quick-hitters or early offense plays because defense is already set up. They can use offensive set plays. Set plays in a check-ball offense are more organized and schematized than those in a transition offense, as teams have more time to prepare and position correctly prior to the beginning of a play.

Teams have options for how to position themselves at the start of the offensive play. Some players form narrow or wide triangles. Some teams start their check-ball offense in a form similar to diagonal line. Each positioning has certain advantages. However, all these tactics require advanced explanations. Let's look at the most basic advantages of different formations if players choose to start their offense with either more inside or more outside presence.

Formations at the start of the check-ball offensive play

3-0 starting formation

The first number refers to the number of players outside the two-point arc and the second number refers to the players inside the two-point arc.

Positioning all three players outside of the two-point arc has some fundamental advantages:

★ It maximizes the space available for driving to the basket.

★ It gives an instant option to all players to make a two-point shot or cut toward the basket.

★ It is suitable for quick, agile players with great dribbling and handling skills who efficiently attack from outside.

But it also comes with fundamental disadvantages:

★ It is hard or sometimes even impossible for a player starting outside the two-point arc to set a perfect screening angle on a pick and roll or to execute an efficient handoff under or just above the two-point arc as professional teams usually deny and obstruct initial movement from offensive players who try to get inside the two-point arc.

★ Players lose energy battling to get to a good position inside the two-point arc.

★ It is not appropriate for teams with players who are slow, are not agile, and don't have adequate dribbling technique. Generally, offensive players need to be able to move great with and without the ball if they decide to position outside the two-point arc at the start of the play.

1-2 and 2-1 starting formation

Teams can also position players on either side of the two-point arc. This too has some fundamental advantages:

★ It enables great pick and rolls and handoffs. It enables a player starting inside the two-point arc to either set efficient pick and roll with a great screening angle or execution of a great handoff under or just above the two-point arc.

★ It enables a team to take advantage of a dominant post player.

★ It enables a player starting inside the two-point arc to reposition and securely receive a ball outside the two-point arc. It is always easier for a player to start inside the two-point arc first and then reposition outside because the defensive player is not obstructing as much, but the other way around is tougher.

★ It puts a player or players in a better position for an offensive rebound or a good initial defensive position.

★ Less time and energy are spent battling to get a good position inside the two-point arc.

But positioning players on either side of the two-point arc also has fundamental disadvantages:

★ Teams need to be particularly careful to use spacing correctly, as positioning is narrower.

★ There is less space available for driving to the basket.

★ It is harder to receive a pass inside the two-point arc, so players need to be pay attention to opportunities to get open without turning the ball over.

★ It is less appropriate if a team is not physically strong and dominant under the basket or if a team is generally avoiding any physical contact due to their playing preferences.

1-2 formation

Team Tactics at the Free-Throw Line

Offensive players need to communicate clearly and structure properly when their teammate is taking free throws in order to know who to guard after play becomes live again. This is extremely important because, after the final allocated free throw, the defensive team will attempt to grab the rebound and quickly clear the ball behind the two-point arc.

When Two Defensive Players Take Position Around the Key

This is the most common positioning at professional games: two defensive players take position around the key and one defensive player waits outside the two-point arc. The best possible and most common positioning of offensive players when their team is at the line is that one player is shooting free throws, a second is taking position on the key, and the third is next to the defensive player outside the two-point arc. After a made or missed free throw, a player outside the two-point arc should deny a pass while the free-throw shooter and the third player communicate about who to guard based on their preference and the situation.

When Three Defensive Players Take Position Around the Key

This positioning is very rare in 3x3, but both offensive players should position around the key if this happens. Even before attempting the last free throw, offensive players should communicate and agree on who to guard. After the final free throw, each player should guard their desired opponent.

When Only One Defensive Player Takes a Position on the Key

This positioning might happen at the end of the game, when a defensive team needs a two-pointer to tie. The defensive team risks losing a defensive rebound with only one defensive player positioned on the key and the other two players outside the two-point arc.

In this case, the two offensive players who aren't shooting should wait outside the two-point arc, each next to one of the opponents. After a made or missed free throw, the shooter covers the defensive player who is recovering the ball while other two offensive players deny their respective opponents a pass.

Team Tactics on Defense

The defensive tactical aim is to prevent the offense from scoring by obstructing movements and denying the execution of offensive plays. A team defense is based on two foundations: The abilities and responsibilities of individuals and mutual cooperation and collective responsibility from the entire team.[29]

Professional 3x3 teams strive to develop a tough and aggressive defense that is the core of their game and can help them overcome sluggish offensive performances, which can often happen in 3x3 since it is a game impacted by outdoor conditions. In transition after a change in possession and before an opponent has cleared the ball, professional teams rely on high-pressure defense to steal as many seconds as possible from the offensive shot clock. In order to execute such defense, teams need to be physically well prepared.

Rules for a Successful 3x3 Defense

I first heard about the Cs of defense at one of Coach David Blatt's seminars. However, I have expanded his seven Cs to 15 to cover the most important and successful defensive strategies in 3x3. The 15 Cs of defense are:

★ **Commit.** Commit to excellence. Give your best!

★ **Communicate.** Communicate E.L.C. (early, loud, and continually).

★ **Concentrate.** Concentrate on every play since the game lasts only 10 minutes. Every play counts.

★ **Convert.** Quickly transition from a successful offense to a successful defense.

★ **Change.** First, box out; second, secure the ball; third, push the ball for quick clearance.

★ **Counter.** Anticipate and successfully read and react to the offensive players.

★ **Contact.** Be aggressive. Don't be afraid of contact.

★ **Compete.** Never give up, because anything is possible in 3x3.

★ **Chase.** Bring energy and chase loose balls. Be the first to 50/50 balls. Hustle!

★ **Conquer.** Conquer the space, and don't give opponents room to rebound or receive a pass.

★ **Contain.** Put pressure on the ball-handler and don't let him penetrate.

★ **Contest.** Keep hands up and active to contest shots and deny passes.

★ **Cover.** Help your teammate or switch when necessary.

★ **Cooperate.** For a defense to be successful, all three players need to coordinate with each other.

★ **Control.** Limit fouling when on defense to control the game's tempo.

The Defensive Tactical Systems

Because there are more players on the court in traditional basketball, there are different defensive tactical systems, such as the zone, mixed, and player-to-player systems. In 3x3, the only viable defensive tactical system is player-to-player—the "man-to-man" defense. A player-to-player defense is a tactical system in which each defensive player covers an assigned offensive player everywhere that player goes on the court to prevent free movement and make it more difficult for the covered player to receive the ball or score. Professional teams regularly apply player-to-player pressure defense in indirect transition. *Crash the offensive glass and press* is a team tactic in which, after transition, a defensive team applies pressure to the offensive team before they clear the ball outside the two-point arc.

In order to successfully execute this tactic, work already starts on offense at the moment a team attempts a shot. First, after the shot, all players should crash the offensive glass as this forces the opponent to box them out. Consequently, every offensive player is now right next to the opponent he will guard once he transitions to defense. So, how to continue the execution of this tactic if an offensive team has scored a basket? After they have made a basket, a defensive team tries to immediately surprise the offensive team so that an on-ball defender obstructs the first pass of the ball-handler who is standing in the semi-circle under the basket while the other two defenders deny the pass. If all defensive players are successful in their tasks, the ball-handler is now forced to dribble. At the moment the ball-handler dribbles the ball out of the semi-circle, the on-ball defender should exert as much on-ball pressure as possible and direct the ball-handler to a corner, while other two defensive players should still deny the pass. The defensive team's goal is to cut down as much time on the shot clock as possible and prevent a quick clearing of the ball. This defensive team tactic is extremely effective against poor ball-handlers and dominant tall players because first, on-ball pressure makes dribbling and passing more difficult, which increases the chances of turnovers, and second, it forces tall players to dribble and clear the ball outside the two-point arc where generally the tallest players are not as dangerous or effective. Once an offensive team has cleared the ball outside the two-point arc, a defensive team should follow their defensive principles. High-level fitness is required to actively exert defensive pressure throughout an entire game. Amateur teams often can't implement these tactics properly because of insufficient high-level training. After a few minutes, their defense will very quickly start to decline. The team tactic called crash the offensive glass and press is further explained later in section: Instructions for a player guarding a ball-handler after a made basket in indirect transition.

Tactical Techniques on Defense

A defensive team can use different tactical techniques when the offense is executing an on-ball screen, a handoff, or other plays. What technique a team opts for depends on their and their opponents' abilities and the location of the offensive play. Switching defense, a tactical technique in which two defenders will change, or "switch," defensive assignments to disrupt the flow of the offense is extremely popular in 3x3. There are far more switches in 3x3 than in traditional basketball because of the game's fast-paced nature and quick transition from offense to defense. Switching defense and pick and roll coverages is explained in chapter 9.

PRACTICAL STEPS, TIPS, AND INSTRUCTIONS

The practical steps and instructions for easier and successful gameplay are presented in this chapter, but a more in-detail explanation of each step will be given in the next chapter.

For an easier and better understanding of the game and in order to give more precise instructions, we can divide both offensive and defensive plays into different subphases that will help us define what players can do to successfully complete plays. I'll focus on the practical classifications, since theory alone can't help a player or coach fully understand what to do in each phase. A transition offense theoretically starts from the moment a defensive team gains possession of the ball in the active phase. However, what a player does when neither of the teams has possession of the ball is just as important, since teams transition from defense to offense very quickly. Generally, the fundamental principles of traditional basketball are the same for 3x3, so I'll only highlight the differences. Players should follow the steps presented in the book as the in-game situations dictate, and they should always read and react to the play.

For a Successful Offense in Indirect Transition

1 A Quick and Efficient Transition from Defense to Offense

This subphase consists of defensive and offensive work from all three players and needs to be carried out in an organized manner. It begins even before the team has acquired possession of the ball on offense and is essential for securing a defensive rebound and kick-starting the next subphase.

Immediately after an opponent has attempted a shot, all three defensive players need to check and box out their assigned opponents or set a good initial offensive position. If a defensive team is successful, they can secure a defensive rebound and then quickly clear the ball outside the two-point arc. However, situations are not always ideal, and even the best defensive teams make mistakes and receive a basket. This subphase is extremely important if this happens. After an opponent has scored a basket and before a defensive team acquires possession of the ball, a player from a non-scoring team should move under the basket to pick up the ball and meanwhile assess the positions of his teammates. At the same time, before their teammate gains a possession, the other two players should reposition and free themselves up from any obstruction or holding to get open outside the two-point arc.

2 A Quick and Efficient Clearance of the Ball

This subphase begins at the moment an offensive team gains the ball. The offensive goal is to quickly and safely clear the ball behind the two-point arc. Fast clearance can leave defenders scrambling and create open shots, easy layups, and mismatches while leaving more time on the shot clock.

After gaining possession, a team must clear the ball outside the two-point arc before they can attempt to score. The clearance is made when a player with the ball has neither feet inside the two-point arc and at least one foot outside the two-point arc. There are three ways to clear the ball: with dribbling, passing, or a combination of these two. A player who gains possession of the ball should always try to make a quick and accurate "clearance" pass outside the two-point arc if at least one teammate is open. Only if passing the ball is not possible should a player dribble the ball outside the two-point arc. Furthermore, it is advisable to dribble and clear the ball at the top or the wing of the two-point arc, avoiding corners and congested spaces. One common tactic for players who aren't great ball-handlers (usually the tallest player on the team) when they acquire the possession but can't pass the ball for a clearance is to dribble the ball directly to a teammate and then execute a handoff above the arc followed by a pick and roll.

3   Carrying Out an Efficient Offensive Play— Attacking the Basket

This subphase starts after the ball has been cleared and scoring attempts are allowed. A transition offense is always designed for players to take advantage of isolations, mismatches, late closeouts, and "two-man" game situations quickly. When the best professional teams are in indirect transition offense, they first try to score as fast as possible with open shots or to take advantage of a mismatch. If they can't do this, they begin other offensive plays—most often pick and rolls and handoffs. Two offensive players work directly in these two plays while the third player serves as a passing or scoring option, maintaining the right spacing in the meantime. Generally, an offensive team should always try to punish the opponent's delay, carelessness, or inflexibility to quickly establish defense in transition.

4   Crashing the Offensive Glass

When a shot is taken, all players should either move to a good position to grab an offensive rebound and have another chance to score or set a good initial defensive position. Any player crashing an offensive board should always be close enough to his or her designated opponent to prevent quick clearance if the defense gains possession.

Instructions for an Offensive Player Who Gains the Ball in Indirect Transition

1. **Box out.** A good transition offense is triggered by a good box out before the team has acquired possession of the ball.

2. **Be aware of the court.** Players should always know where the ball and their teammates are.

3. **Gather the ball.** A player can gain possession of the ball through a rebound, through a steal, or by quickly picking up the ball after a basket. Players can always dictate the tempo when they have the ball, and that is based on the scoreboard and time remaining. When teams wish to slow the tempo after they receive a basket, they may stand in the no-charge circle rather than move quickly beyond the two-point arc. Slowing the tempo is important for a number of reasons, such as to stop the other team's momentum and to defend a lead.

4. **Pass the ball out for clearance.** A player should first look to pass the ball to an open teammate beyond the two-point arc. The pass should be made quickly and accurately to reduce the risk of turnovers. If options are limited, passes should be made to the top or the wing, as it is vital to avoid corners and congested areas. If passing isn't possible, dribble the ball beyond the two-point arc. A ball-handler should dribble quick and low, protecting the ball. Players should avoid dribbling to corners or through congested areas. Finally, a dribbler should not instantly hold the ball after clearing it without knowing what to do next.

5. **Be an instant offensive threat.** A player who has passed the ball from under the basket should immediately try to seal the defender and prepare to receive a pass straight back into the key. Importantly, a player should always be aggressive toward the basket and look for a way for the team to score.

6. **Free up from a defender.** A player should free up from an opponent's holding or obstruction and maintain free movement.

7. **Move without the ball and generate team movement.** Players should use changes of directions and other skills, always moving to the most favorable position to either receive a pass or make an offensive play. While moving, players should mind their spacing!

8. **Conquer the space.** Players should always try to conquer as much space as possible by getting into a good position to either receive the ball or secure a rebound. A low and stable basketball stance enables those players to fight to out-position defenders.

9. **Set off-ball screens.** A player should set off-ball screens. (This and the following steps will be explained in greater detail in the next chapter.)

10. **Set pick and rolls and handoffs, and use other plays involving two or more players.** Not just passing but also fundamental plays such as pick and rolls and handoffs are extremely important for success in 3x3.

11. **Finish the offensive play.** A player and a team should look for the best position from which to take a shot and score.

12. **Crash the offensive glass.**

Can a Bad Defense Lead to a Successful Transition Offense?

Sometimes, a transition offense can be effective even when the defense was bad. For example, a player who is blown by or who has failed a defensive task can quickly reposition outside the two-point arc before an offense has scored a basket. As soon as a basket is made, the newly offensive team can get the ball back to that player, who will now be outside the two-point arc and possibly unmarked. With quick execution, sloppy defensive plays can be rectified in the offensive exchange.

For a Successful Offense in Direct Transition

Because a team has gained possession outside the two-point arc, the successful indirect transition offense does not have a subphase of quick and efficient ball clearance. This means there is less offensive work as a team is allowed to immediately shoot on the basket. Tips and instructions for a successful offense in direct transition are the same as those in indirect transition except for those tips and instructions which apply for a quick and efficient clearance of the ball.

Subphases of successful transition offense:

1. A quick and efficient transition from defense to offense

2. Carrying out an efficient offensive play—attacking the basket

3. Crashing the offensive glass

For a Successful Offense in Check-ball Phase

Offensive players in a check-ball offense have more time to position and organize themselves at the start of the offensive play, so their gameplay and tactics should be more organized than in a transition phase. Moreover, teams have more time to complete the offensive play because they don't need to clear the ball before they are allowed to attempt a shot, as in an indirect transition. This means that a check-ball offense can be thoroughly prepared with set movements and plays.

1   Arrangement of Players

This subphase occurs in the passive phase. It happens when the ball is dead and lasts until the completion of the check-ball. The goal of the offensive players in this subphase is to arrange on the court in such a way that the team can start their offensive set play with the correct spacing, width, and balance.

The shot clock can't start running before the check-ball is complete, so it is essential for the checking player to take his or her time. A checking player during a passive phase should not immediately give the ball to the defender but only after confirming that teammates are ready. All three offensive players need to know what play they are using before the play begins. At the beginning of the passive phase, there should be verbal or non-verbal communication with teammates so everyone is on the same page. This buys players time to position themselves correctly. One of the biggest mistakes is to call set plays when the check-ball is already complete.

2   Carrying Out an Efficient Offensive Play—Attacking the Basket

This subphase starts after the check-ball is complete and the previous dead ball becomes live. Professional 3x3 teams execute principles-based or schematic plays in this phase.

3   Crashing the Offensive Glass

When shots are attempted, players should either crash the offensive board to get an offensive rebound or set a good initial defensive position inside the two-point arc.

For a Successful Defense in Indirect Transition

1   Quick and Efficient Transition From Offense to Defense

This subphase happens even before an opponent has acquired possession of the ball and consists of both defensive and offensive "work" from all players. It needs to be carried out in an organized manner.

Once one of the teammates attempts a shot, the whole team should reposition under the two-point arc and communicate, organize, and establish before an opponent has acquired possession. This is done either by crashing the offensive glass or repositioning players inside the two-point arc to be ready to play denial defense and obstruct player movement. It is important to note that, after a score, defenders cannot guard opponents in the protected semicircle under the basket until they dribble or pass the ball out of the semicircle.

Who to Guard After a Made Basket?

Most often in professional 3x3 games, the scoring player guards the player recovering the ball under the basket, who was likely the scoring player's defender prior to the score. The other two players transitioning to defense will guard their closest opponents or the biggest scoring threat. Team communication is essential to ensure everyone is on the same page.

Can an Easy Basket Lead to a Bad Transition Defense?

Teams will always face defensive dilemmas. For example, it is hard to know whom the player driving to the basket should guard once his or her defensive player has repositioned to the two-point arc to transition to offense. In a common tactic, a defender will let a player drive, taking advantage of the opportunity to quickly reposition outside the two-point arc. It looks like bad defense, but it is intentional, allowing the defender to move to a strong attacking position.

How can you combat this player who is suddenly ready for a dangerous counterattack? When the defense gives up a basket like this, one off-ball player on the offense should anticipate and shift to defensive mode, moving to guard the open player through a denial defense and preventing late closeouts or open shots. The scorer should also quickly pivot to defense by obstructing the fast clearance pass. The most common mistake beginner teammates of the scoring player make in this situation is staying with the opponents who had been guarding them. Instead, teammates should anticipate and be ready to guard an opponent outside the two-point arc and let the scorer guard a player who will pick up the ball after a made basket. This is a prime example of why defenders need to be able to guard multiple players in the transition phase. Players have to always be forward-looking and ready for defense, even when they are in the flow of their offense.

2   Denying the Quick and Efficient Ball Clearance

This subphase starts once the new offense gains the ball. Defenders should force opponents to run down the shot clock before clearing the ball. These are the fundamental rules for a successful second subphase:

★   On-ball defender should obstruct a pass from the ball-handler.

★   Off-ball defenders should deny a pass to the other offensive players.

★   Obstruct any free movement by the offensive players.

★   Apply pressure defense to a ball-handler who chooses to dribble.

★   Direct a ball-handler to corners or to the most congested areas to prevent a fast transition outside the two-point arc. (Fan the ball.)

3 Denying the Successful Execution of the Offensive play

After an offense has cleared the ball, the defensive team tries to prevent organized offensive plays, penetration inside the two-point arc, open passes, open shots, and free movement of offensive players.

4 Securing a Defensive Rebound

This phase prevents offensive rebounds and is fundamental for quick and efficient transition to offense. Every defensive player should first check and then box out an opponent who is crashing an offensive glass.

Instructions for a Player Guarding a Ball-Handler After a Made Basket in Indirect Transition

1. **Set a good initial defensive position.** After a shot attempt, a player on offense should either hit the glass for an offensive rebound or think defensively and reposition between the basket and an opponent who might become an offensive threat.

2. **Be aware of the court.** It is important to know where every player is on the court while keeping focused on the ball. Court awareness should be maintained during the entire defense.

3. **Communicate.** Communication between teammates is important and should be constant.

4. **Force a dribble instead of a pass.** The player should "jam" the rebounder by stepping close (around the semicircle) with arms outstretched and obstruct the pass. The goal is to slow or prevent the pass rather than steal the ball.

5. **Fan the ball.** Once the ball-handler dribbles the ball outside the no-guard zone, a an on-ball defensive player should be in a low and stable defensive stance between the two-point arc and the ball-handler. A defender should force the dribbler into corners or the most congested area on the court and not allow dribbling to the top of the two-point arc, instead allowing movement in width (toward the baseline and sideline).

6. **Apply on-ball pressure.** A player should apply aggressive pressure on the ball-handler with the goal of stealing the ball or running down the shot clock by obstructing free offensive movement.

7. **Reposition.** A defensive player should reposition between a ball-handler and the basket just moments before the ball has been cleared.

8. **Follow defensive team principles.** After the offense has cleared the ball and ball-handler chooses to pass, a defensive player should jump to the ball to deny any front cuts and apply denial defense, still in low defensive stance.

For Successful Defense in a Direct Transition

Because an opponent has gained possession outside the two-point arc, the successful direct transition defense does not have a subphase of denying the quick and efficient ball clearance. All tips and instructions for a successful defense in direct transition are the same as those in indirect transition except for those tips and instructions which apply to denying the quick and efficient ball clearance.

Subphases of successful direct transition defense:

1. Quickly and efficiently transitioning from offense to defense.

2. Denying the successful execution of the offensive play.

3. Securing a defensive rebound.

Practical Steps and Tips for Successful Defense in Check-ball Phase

Subphases of successful check-ball defense:

1. Arranging players.

2. Denying the successful execution the offensive play.

3. Securing a defensive rebound.

From the first subphase when the ball is dead until the check-ball is complete, defensive players should properly set up and arrange. The defensive player who is checking the ball should not exchange the ball with offensive player before he ensures his teammates are ready to play. Compared to transition defense, a check-ball defense is more similar to traditional basketball since players can select whom they want to guard and have time to get into position. After the check-ball is complete and the ball is live, defensive players should follow the principles and instructions presented in the next chapter.

CHAPTER 9
FUNDAMENTALS AND PRINCIPLES

The fundamental 3x3 principles, steps, and plays necessary for a successful 3x3 game will be presented and explained in this chapter. However, it is important to gauge whether teams are using certain plays (technical–tactical elements), such as handoffs, as the beginning or end of their offense. In both 3x3 and traditional basketball, the basic principles of both offense and defense are the same, and the more advanced principles are similar. However, there are few rule differences that lead to a unique style of play in 3x3.

FUNDAMENTALS AND PRINCIPLES ON OFFENSE

Crashing the Offensive Glass

In 3x3, after a shot attempt, every offensive player should crash the offensive glass. This unique principle is opposite to what guards are used to in traditional basketball where they need to defend fast breaks. Generally, every player in traditional basketball who crashes the offensive boards is one less player who can get back on defense. However, this is not the case in 3x3 where a game is played only on one basket. So, why exactly should an offensive player outside the two-point arc crash the offensive glass in 3x3?

First, 3x3 is an outdoor game, shooting can sometimes be affected by the outdoor conditions and securing an offensive rebound can create valuable extra opportunities for scoring. Second, by doing that, a player repositions under the two-point arc and contests the rebound which forces a defensive player to box him out. Now an offensive player is right next to player he will defend if an opponent acquires the possession of the ball. This enables a player to quickly and efficiently transition from offense to defense. When it comes to crashing the offensive glass during the game, there should be a tactic behind this because 3x3 transition happens so quickly that you might be required to suddenly defend. Generally, an offensive player should crash the offensive glass at such that he is still close enough to a player he will guard once he transitions to defense.

Setting a Good Initial Defensive Position

Sometimes offensive players don't crash the offensive glass due to fatigue or other reasons. Those offensive players should instead set a good initial defensive position as this will enable efficient denial defense and prevent quick clearance by an opponent. Therefore, an offensive player's goal right after taking a shot and deciding to not crash the glass is to reposition (when neither team has possession) so as to get inside the two-point arc and next to an opponent he or she will guard.

Freeing Up From a Defender

Due to the physical nature of 3x3, offensive players without the ball must break free from opponents' holding and obstructing to open the passing lane and get the ball. Because moving without the ball is critical, it is important to be aware that a defensive player can easily obstruct initial movement and bump or hold an offensive player who is standing. However, an offensive player who is already moving can make faster and more efficient direction changes (gain space), making it harder for a defensive player to hold or obstruct. Smaller and less physical players should move immediately after transitioning to offense to prevent highly physical defenders from obstructing their initial movement.

Moving Without the Ball and Generating Team Movement

While ball movement is extremely important and can be accomplished through passing, moving without the ball is a commonly overlooked but crucial aspect of a 3x3 offense. Learning and perfecting the habit in training is necessary. 3x3 players should always share the ball and have a constant flow of movement on offense to create multiple attacking options while avoiding unnecessary dribbling, which is dangerous given the high level of contact, less time on the shot clock, and opponents' pressure defense. Passing needs to be extremely accurate in order to minimize turnovers, and the ball-handler needs to frequently target a "shot pocket" so a teammate can receive a quality pass and take a quick and open shot. In addition to all these factors, moving without the ball is important because there are only two players on the court who can potentially receive the ball.

To be efficient, players without the ball use different cuts. A properly executed cut helps a player get open and receive the ball or draws away defensive players to allow teammates to score. V-cuts, backdoor cuts, front cuts, and curl cuts are just some of the examples of the most used maneuvers in 3x3. In traditional basketball, shooters such as Stephen Curry frequently make deep cuts to use a static screen near the keyway to get open for a shot. In 3x3, those cuts are not as deep, as a screener is usually standing near the two-point arc and very rarely close to the keyway. Other frequently used and efficient 3x3 cuts are shuffle cuts, where a player cuts from one side of the court and goes to the other side in one quick action. This dramatically shifts the spread of players both offensively and defensively.

These are the ways a player can effectively move without the ball:

★ **Stay active and keep moving.** Standing still gives the defense a chance to recover. Moving without the ball makes defenders tired and creates scoring opportunities. Constantly moving and creating offensive scoring options for the team doesn't show up in the statistics, but its value is immense.

★ **Change speed and direction.** A moving player should accelerate and decelerate and change directions multiple times to leave the defender guessing and gain space to receive the ball.

★ **Change sides and find open space.** Don't move on only one side of the court. A player should break away from defenders to cut to open spaces.

★ **Mind the spacing.** Cuts have to be made at a proper angle and with proper spacing, giving teammates adequate room and allowing more efficient movement. This makes defenders work harder and makes it difficult for them to implement help defense.

Conquering the Space

Conquering space is vital because 3x3 has much more room on the court than traditional basketball. Offensive players need to conquer ("cover") more area inside the two-point arc than defensive players to get good positioning to receive or rebound the ball. Physical strength can help players achieve this. Moreover, good positioning and conquering more area than an opponent helps to draw fouls and also leads to easy buckets under the basket. For players to successfully receive the ball inside the paint, they need to:

★ be in a low and stable stance.

★ make a "drop" step in front of the defender.

★ duck in and seal.

★ reach out a hand and signal where a teammate should pass the ball.

★ hold position until receiving the pass.

Screening

On-ball and off-ball screens are one of the most important offensive plays in 3x3. Players should know how to set, use, and read screens to be successful, all of which can be slightly different than in traditional basketball. Second, it is important that all three players make either on- or off-ball screens, and not just the tallest players, which enables more attack options. This might be different from what basketball guards are used to.

Karlis Lasmanis and Nauris Miezis from the 2020 FIBA 3x3 World Tour Championship team Riga are masters in cutting.

Duck in and seal.

Off-Ball Screens

Off-ball screening is a practice of the best 3x3 teams. It forces movement from the two offensive players without the ball, which can lead to a pass from the third player. Screen away, back screen, flare screen, and down screen are some of the most used off-ball screens in 3x3. Moreover, the best 3x3 shooters and scorers are also off-ball screening masters, as it enables them to get open or gain advantage after a late defensive switch.

On-Ball Screens

On-ball screens ("picks") are one of the simplest offensive plays and can be very difficult to defend against when done correctly, but they require synergy between all teammates. A dynamic duo that is great at executing picks or handoffs is extremely hard and sometimes impossible to stop. Professional teams use picks frequently because the right execution can lead to a mismatch, an open driving lane, an open jump shot, an open layup, or even an open shot from a third player.

Importantly, picks are used and executed slightly differently in 3x3 than in traditional basketball. When traditional basketball players and 3x3 players execute picks, the screener needs to be stationary at the moment of contact with the on-ball defender. Leaning in, moving, or extending the arms is a rule violation ("illegal screening") in both disciplines. However, since 3x3 is more physical, 3x3 referees call illegal screening less often and less readily than in traditional basketball. Because of that, 3x3 screeners can use more contact and can move more quickly into the "roll" or "pop" compared to traditional basketball. Thus, screeners should take advantage and adjust on-ball screening execution, moving to make a contact and obtain an advantage. In the early years of professional 3x3, isolation plays and pick and rolls were common. However, tightening rules about moving screens and pushing on screens in 2018 lead to a decline in the frequency of pick and rolls and an increase in handoffs. Teams started to use isolation less and incorporate different team plays in which all players shared the ball and were more equally involved.

3x3 Screen Characteristics

The fundamentals of on- and off-ball screening are:

★ **Position.** On-ball screens should be set right under or on the two-point arc if possible. It is advisable to do on-ball screens on top or on the wings, avoiding corners.

★ **Angle:** Screening angle is extremely important, with the screener needing a low and stable stance. Horizontally set on-ball screens are common feature of the NBA teams, but in 3x3 a screener should set a more diagonal on-ball screen on top and the middle of the two-point arc. These are the most efficient because:

    − It is harder for an on-ball defender to go under a pick.

    − Screeners are in a better position to seal a switching defender.

    − Screeners can roll much faster.

★ **Possible screens.** Re-screens, fake screens, and slip screens are frequently used and extremely effective in 3x3 due to switching defenses. Moreover, professional teams use a lot of shuffle screens, with the screener coming from one side of the court and then setting a screen on the other side. A highly effective pick and roll is when a screener changes the angle or direction of the screen at the last second. Last but not least, blind screen, in which a defensive player does not see a screen coming and is therefore caught off guard, is also extremely efficient.

★ **Dynamic screens:** Dynamic screens, in which screeners move to set their screens, are more effective and more frequently used by professional 3x3 teams than stationary screens.

FIBA 3x3 World Tour MVP 2019 Dominque Jones in action during the pick and roll play.

The best strategy against a switching defense is to exploit a mismatch; however, this might not be always possible as some teams have four versatile defenders on their roster. So, how to execute a pick and roll on the top of the two-point arc when a defensive team is using a switching defense?

It is more complex, but here are the fundamentals:

★ Screener sets a good angle for the pick right under or at the two-point arc. This forces the defense to switch.

★ On the pick and roll, the ball-handler dribbles one step wide (in) and one step up. This draws a defending player to make a switch higher to prevent an open two-point shot.

★ The screener should set a quick and strong re-pick in the opposite direction as the first on-ball screen and at a diagonal, forcing the defense to switch again.

★ The ball-handler should use a re-pick and drive while the screener quickly slips or rolls. This time, the switch will be late, and the defense will be caught off guard if the timing and execution of the re-pick is right.

Why Are Dynamic Screens Better?

Dynamic screens are more effective and more frequently used by 3x3 teams than stationary screens. In dynamic screens, the screener moves toward the screen, enabling a faster change of angle or direction. The defender is less prepared for what will transpire next, as the screener can effectively make a slip or fake screen. This helps the screener gain more space from the defender than in a static screen. The best shooters in traditional basketball, like Steph Curry, are constantly moving to get into open scoring positions, and that template is the same in 3x3—albeit with more physicality allowed, which makes it harder to get into desired spots. However, the screener is a major contrast between traditional basketball and 3x3. The screener in traditional basketball, usually the center, is sometimes standing still while the target player is cutting. In a 3x3 offense, a screen should be dynamic, as the screener should move and come to set a screen, which requires perfect timing. Due to the physical nature of 3x3, it's harder to get good stable position for screening. Therefore, the screener should first get free from an opponent, move toward the ball-handler and only then find the right angle for the screen in a stable position.

Handoffs

Handoff, a play where the ball-handler hands the ball to a teammate, is alongside the on-ball screen as a key part of professional 3x3 offenses. There are certain advantages to both dribble and non-dribble handoffs. A non-dribble handoff, in which the player executing a handoff has not yet dribbled, is extremely hard to guard due to the switching nature of defense. Importantly, while two offensive players are executing pick and rolls or handoffs, the third player should keep spacing to help the execution.

The fundamentals of a handoff in 3x3 are:

★ **Position:** The best position for a handoff is with the ball-handler inside the two-point arc and the receiving teammate just above the two-point arc. Players should set handoffs at the wing or top of the two-point arc—not in the corners.

★ **Non-dribble handoffs:** Non-dribble handoffs are extremely effective against switching defenses. They give players an option to fake a handoff (in case defenses switch) and drive to the basket.

★ **Handoff and pick:** If a player chooses to make a dribble handoff, it is extremely effective to follow it with a pick and roll.

The best professional teams frequently execute "screen handoff," which makes offenses more dangerous and harder to thwart. This two-player play is different from a pick and roll, in which a screener without the ball is setting an on-ball screen. In a screen handoff, a player with the ball serves as a screener, obstructing an off-ball defender with his or her body, then hands off the ball when a teammate is in position to score or receive the ball, and lastly rolls, pops, or seals a defender, which contrasts with a simple handoff in which the ball is immediately dished off. If executed correctly, screen handoffs open up the chance for two-point shots.

The best position for a handoff is with the ball-handler inside the two-point arc and the receiving teammate just above the two-point arc.

FUNDAMENTALS AND PRINCIPLES ON DEFENSE

One-on-One Defense

One-on-one defense on the ball-handler is critical, as defenders must be able to curtail a dribbler with limited help defense. The principles are the same to those of traditional basketball, as a defensive player should always be close to the ball-handler in a such manner that he or she can't dribble freely around the court and take an uncontested shot. However, when 3x3 defenders are outplayed, they should either

★ lock on the hip and influence a ball-handler's path away from a layup;

★ quickly reposition over the two-point arc even before an opponent has scored a basket so they can quickly receive the ball once they transition to offense; or

★ make a foul on mismatch to prevent a made basket.

Lock on the hip.

Off-Ball Denial Defense

Professional 3x3 players tend to either play half-side overplay denial defense on low block or let offensive players get the ball, but not in a beneficial scoring position. Defenders choose not to front on low block as in traditional basketball because:

★   it leaves more open space between an offensive player and the basket.

★   defenders are more vulnerable to being out-positioned by an offensive player.

★   an offensive player might be in a better position to grab an offensive rebound.

Securing a Defensive Rebound

All three players on defense are responsible for boxing out their opponents to get them out of a possible rebounding situation. Since there is a lot of open space, defensive players should cover all possible routes by which the ball might rebound off the rim. Which defensive player rebounds the ball doesn't really matter.

When an opponent has attempted a shot, defensive players should check the opponent, box him or her out, be well-balanced, maintain contact, and immediately face toward the basket. It is extremely important to maintain full contact with an opponent so he or she doesn't have a chance to maneuver the body to a better position. As presented before in the findings of the discriminant analysis of the 2019 and 2020 3x3 World Tour season, there was a significant discrimination between winners and losers when it came to defensive rebounds. Defensive rebounds reduce an opponent's extra scoring chances on one hand and on the other they open up a possibility of the quick-hitter plays. Compared to traditional basketball, 3x3 characteristics such as the outside conditions, more running from the two-point arc to grab rebounds, and fewer players who can potentially grab a rebound magnify the importance of correctly boxing out and securing a rebound.

Box out and rebound.

Defending On-Ball Screens at the Top and Outside the Two-Point Arc

A successful defense against on-ball screens depends on the coordinated action of at least two players. Communication is vital. Depending on the game situation and location of the screen, defensive teams can use different coverages when defending on-ball screens. In the early days of 3x3, professional teams used mostly switching defense, but currently teams defend against picks based on an opponent's ability to score two-pointers and their ability to exploit mismatches.

Drop Coverage and Follow

Modern 3x3 teams defend picks against great two-point shooting teams with a drop coverage from a player guarding a screener and where the player guarding the ball-handler follows and goes over the screen. These tactics are designed to prevent open two-pointers from a ball-handler and force elbow shots or contested layups.

When the offense is executing a pick and roll, the player defending the screener drops and meets the ball-handler at or below the screen so that the ball-handler can't freely drive or shoot. This defender is responsible for both the screener and the ball-handler until the ball-handler's defender gets back in front or next to his or her original opponent. It is vital that a defender guarding a screener is dropping in a low defensive stance, forcing the ball-handler retreat and use a weak hand if possible. At the same time, this defender should be careful and prepared to backpedal in order to prevent a screener getting a position behind him or her which would result in a pass and easy layup. Balancing these tasks takes a lot of skill and discipline.

Meanwhile the player guarding a ball-handler locks and trails the ball-handler while going over the screener. This defender has to get back to guarding the ball-handler as quickly as possible.

Robbie Hummel, 2019 FIBA 3x3 World Cup gold medalist:

"Our strategy is in pick and roll; the big is back and the guard goes over the top. I start with that because our philosophy is if a team is making 21 pull-ups or 21 tough contested layups, we are going to make enough two-pointers. It's an analytics thing."[39]

Drop coverage and follow.

Under, Under-Two

These two defense forms on a pick and roll, where the on-ball defender goes under the screener or both the screener and his teammate and then meets and guards the ball-handler on the other side of the screen, are very popular in 3x3 amateur competitions. They are most effective against a ball-handler who isn't a great two-point shooter. Since there are very few poor shooters at the Pro Circuit, these two defense forms are less commonly used among professionals.

Icing and Rejecting a Pick and Roll

Due to the higher degree of physical contact and more open space in 3x3, rejecting picks is not as common a tactic as in traditional basketball. Making sure that a ball-handler does not use the screen but instead directing him away from the screen at the top of the two-point arc would allow a ball-handler an open driving line to a basket and less possible help in the key. Even if a player guarding a screener drops and helps, this leaves space for a screener to pop-out and get alone on the two-point arc.

However, 3x3 teams can effectively use ice defense on wing picks. In this strategy, a defender prevents a ball-handler coming to the middle of the floor and forces the ball-handler to drive and take an elbow shot. The defender guarding the screener should drop to prevent an open drive and, when the teammate on the ball-handler signals that he or she can guard the ball-handler again, quickly return to guarding the screener. The ice defense on wing picks is a good tactic to implement if the screener is not a good shooter.

Hard Hedge and Recover, Trap

In traditional basketball, some coaches demand a hard hedge and recover coverage from a defender guarding a screener, which forces the dribbler out high. Moreover, some teams double-team the ball-handler. These two tactics are not common in 3x3 because the third defensive player can't help and stack the paint without leaving his assigned player alone. This leads to an open area under the basket where a screener can roll, receive the pass, and make an open layup.

Switching Defense on Pick and Rolls

Switching defense is most common in the last minutes of the game, when players are exhausted, and the intensity and quality of the defense deteriorates. If a defensive team doesn't have versatile players on their roster and still chooses to switch all screens, an opponent will try to exploit mismatches. However, at the same time, switching defense has positive features such as it disrupts the offensive flow, prevents any straight-line drives to the rim, and can also be used against great two-point shooting teams; but it is difficult to implement correctly.

These are the fundamental rules of switching defense for the defender who guards the screener:

★ Before the offensive player sets a screen, communication with the defender getting screened is vital. Make a call so your teammate will know a screen is coming.

★ Get in screener's path. Be physical and obstruct screener movement.

★ Let your teammate know you are switching.

★ Push a screener before he or she sets a screen to get the him or her off balance, allowing a teammate to switch under.

★ Aggressively switch on the ball-handler.

★ Stop the ball-handler's momentum so the ball-handler retreats a dribble.

★ Force a weak hand.

These are the fundamental rules of switching defense for a defender who guards ball-handler:

★ Communication with your teammate is vital. Listen for the call from your teammate. When you hear it, be aware that a screen is coming and that you'll be switching.

★ Press the ball and force the ball-handler to do extra work before the screen happens.

★ Anticipate the screening angle and adjust the direction of your stance.

★ Right before the screen happens retreat so you will be able to go under the screen.

★ Switch on a screener while going under him.

★ Prevent an unobstructed roll or seal.

CHAPTER 10
THE LAST CHAPTER

FIBA 3X3'S STRUCTURE

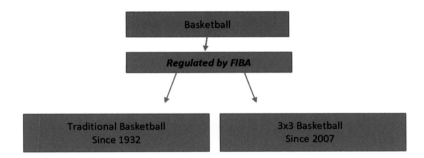

The International Basketball Federation, more commonly known by the French acronym FIBA (Fédération Internationale de Basketball), is the world governing body for basketball. The association consists of various national organizations and oversees various basketball competitions. It was founded by eight nations in 1932 and now brings together 213 national basketball federations worldwide. Since 3x3's birth, this new, exciting discipline is well represented in the organization. 3x3 is represented on the FIBA management team by the FIBA 3x3 managing director and has further representation through the FIBA 3x3 Commission, which consist of former and current 3x3 players, officials, national federations representatives, and private organizers. The first chairman of this commission is ex-NBA All-Star Andrei Kirilenko. 3x3 is managed and operated by FIBA 3x3, a dedicated business unit run out of the House of Basketball in Mies, Switzerland. FIBA 3x3 is responsible for governing the international competition of 3x3 and organizing competitions and other events with the goal of further promoting the sport of basketball around the world.

Andrei Kirilenko, ex-NBA All-Star:

"I started my career as a basketballer playing outside on the street with my friends. 3x3 aligns with my life principles and I am very happy to be part of this commission and help to continue to grow and develop 3x3 around the world."[40]

PATRICK BAUMANN

Patrick Baumann can be credited as the mastermind and driving force behind FIBA's 3x3 vision, and his strong leadership was instrumental in 3x3 securing its coveted Olympic status. For 16 years, Patrick Baumann was FIBA's Secretary General—a title he held until he passed away by heart attack during the 2018 Youth Olympic Games in Buenos Aires. But his legacy will endure, and particularly the spark he lit that allowed 3x3 to become a global phenomenon.

In the hot seat, Baumann was a man of action, focusing primarily on the global development of the youth sector and 3×3—two elements he considered key to achieving the lofty goal of basketball overtaking soccer as the world's most popular sport by the 2028 Los Angeles Olympics.[41] To achieve this ambitious goal, Baumann believed appealing to the youth was key and that 3x3 could aid this by being a game that could easily translate globally. His vision included 3x3 developing with the help of private promoters instead of federations—a philosophy that countered FIBA's traditional approach. After Baumann's unexpected passing, FIBA renamed its headquarters the Patrick Baumann House of Basketball in December 2018 to honor his memory and his sizeable contributions to the sport and its disciplines.

Patrick Baumann.

ONE FINAL THOUGHT

Writing the first book about 3x3 has been a privilege, especially because this game has given me so much, and I believe it will provide a wealth of knowledge for all those interested. Moreover, undertaking this project has been an immense responsibility, and I have tried to simply document and present the most important aspects of 3x3—a game still unknown to many people. Writing the book took a great deal of time and energy, as there is not extensive existing literature and research on the topic, and not many specific definitions, classifications, or explanations of 3x3 terms, tactics, or game structure. This is in contrast to basketball, which has been researched and published on. All this led me to believe that a book about 3x3 was needed.

3x3 has evolved rapidly since its first international event in 2010, and its future looks incredibly bright. The Covid-19 pandemic in 2020 has been a speedbump for the sport, as it has derailed almost every aspect of daily life. 3x3 has not been immune to this, but this great game has the foundation to get back on track. It will undoubtedly receive a big burst of momentum after the Olympics and will hopefully continue to spread to all parts of the globe—which has been FIBA's vision from the start. I believe more countries will form professional 3x3 leagues in the future and that the professionalization of the sport will become more established. But only time will tell.

I have to thank everyone who made this book possible and helped me on this path. Special thanks to FIBA 3x3, 3x3.EXE Premier, 3BL, and the former owners of the Tachikawa Dice, who helped make this book possible. Thank you to all athletes, coaches, referees, and officials who shared important 3x3 details that were not yet known to the public. Thank you to Dušan Bulut, Milan Isakov, Danilo Lukić, and the others who gave interviews and shared their knowledge and experience. Special thanks to Mr. Julien Debove and all the others from FIBA 3x3 who helped me with this project during the unprecedented COVID-19 pandemic by sharing their historical and statistical data, which represented the foundation of this book. Thanks also to Mr. Marko Radovanović, head of global scouting for the Houston Rockets, and those who took time to read and give feedback on this book. I can't shout out everyone who contributed, but please know I have valued your input.

3x3 is more than just a game; it's a labor of love for anyone who has played it and a wonderful community. I want to urge everyone reading this book who has not watched or played 3x3 to start—you won't be disappointed. It is really fun and not difficult to learn. 3x3 is no longer the "other" basketball game. It's a game of its own with an already rich history—and the journey has only just started.

REFERENCES

1. "The NBA All Star bringing B-ball to B-town."Interview by Birmingham 2022. https://www.birmingham2022.com/news/blog/3x3-basketball-atsmithfield/

2. Frane Erčulj. "Metodika učenja košarkarskih iger na en koš." Revija Šport (2013): 13–20.

3. B. T. McCormick et al. "Comparison of Physical Activity in Small-Sided Basketball Games Versus Full-Sided Games." *International Journal of Sports Science and Coaching* 7 (2012): 689–97.

4. B. Mitreva. "3x3 Basketball Training in Higher Education Institutions." Sofia, Bulgaria: Sofia University, 2015.

5. Jaime Sampaio, Catarina Abrantes, and Nuno Leite. "Power, Heart Rate and Perceived Exertion Responses to 3x3 and 4x4 Basketball Small-Sided Games." *Revista de Psicologia del Deporte* 18 (2009): 463–46.

6. Filipe M. Clemente. "Small-Sided and Conditioned Games in Basketball Training." *Strength and Conditioning Journal* 38 (2016): 49–58

7. Sergio Fernandez-Martinez et al. "Incidence of Type of Game Mode in Player Participation in Minibasket." *Revista de Psicologia del Deporte* 24 (2015): 656–68.

8. Isabel Piñar et al. "Participation of Minibasketball Players During Small-Sided Competitions." *Revista de Psicología del Deporte* 18 (2009): 445–49.

9. Isabel Tallir et al. "Learning Opportunities in 3 on 3 versus 5 on 5 Basketball Game Play: An Application of Nonlinear Pedagogy." *International Journal of Sport Psychology* 43 (2012): 420–37.

10. "Authorized Access - Julius Randle at Dew NBA 3X in Los Angeles." Interview by Brandon Armstrong. NBA. October 22, 2017. Video. https://www.youtube.com/watch?v=KZWKlpwQ_Eg.

11. "US rising star Zach Collins looks back on unique 3x3 experience." Interview by FIBA.basketball. July 19, 2017. http://www.fiba.basketball/en/news/us-rising-star-zach-collins-looks-back-on-unique-3x3-experience.

12. "NBA rising star Hollis-Jefferson: 'I would love to play 3x3 again'." Interview by FIBA.basketball. October 15, 2018. https://www.fiba.basketball/news/nba-rising-star-hollis-jefferson-i-would-love-to-play-3x3-again.

13. "McKinnie: '3x3 has helped me grow as a leader'." Interview by FIBA.basketball. April 3, 2017. http://www.fiba.basketball/3x3worldcup/2017/news/mckinnie-3x3-has-helped-me-grow-as-a-leader.

14. "'3x3 helps us get tougher!' | Sabrina Ionescu (Team USA)." FIBA 3x3. Video. https://youtu.be/zM5uoMyXLVs.

15. "3x3 – Ponkrashov salutes 'great experience' playing 3x3." FIBA.basketball. July 17, 2013. http://www.fiba.basketball/news/3x3-Ponkrashov-salutes--great-experience--playing-3x3.

16. "3x3 – Garbajosa highlights VIP game at Czech House." FIBA.basketball. August 10, 2012. http://www.fiba.basketball/news/3x3-Garbajosa-highlights-VIP-game-at-Czech-House.

17. Chris Palmer. Streetball: *All the Ballers, Moves, Slams and Shine.* New York: HarperCollins, 2004.

18. "New York Streetball - Played real hard." Trailer for *Doin' It In the Park.* May 31, 2013. Video. https://www.youtube.com/watch?v=opGiIryUsIc.

19. "LaMelo Ball says he's such a good rebounder because he played a lot of twenty-one | The Jump." ESPN. January 11, 2021. Video. https://www.youtube.com/watch?v=5snoOF5TkaI

20. "Historic day for basketball as 3x3 added to Olympic Program." FIBA.basketball. June 9, 2017. https://www.fiba.basketball/news/historic-day-for-basketball-as-3x3-added-to-olympic-program.

21. "Why Former NBA Star Stephon Marbury Has Deep Appreciation for 3x3." FIBA.Basketball. March 22, 2019. https://worldtour.fiba3x3.com/2019/news/why-former-nba-star-stephon-marbury-has-deep-appreciation-for-3x3.

22. "FIBA – Organisers lay court for inaugural Youth Olympic 3on3 basketball." FIBA. basketball. August 2, 2010. http://www.fiba.basketball/news/FIBA---Organisers-lay-court-for-inaugural-Youth-Olympic-3on3-basketball.

23. "3x3 Basketball Youth Olympic Games." FIBA 3x3. July 21, 2011. Video. https://www.youtube.com/watch?v=RcHBTrOpmbM.

24. "PR N° 12 – FIBA launches revolutionary digital platform 3x3planet.com." FIBA.basketball. June 13, 2012. http://www.fiba.basketball/news/PR-N--12-FIBA-launches-revolutionary-digital-platform-3x3planet-com.

25. "LeBron James' dream 3x3 team: Jordan, Magic and himself." FIBA. basketball. June 12, 2017. http://www.fiba.basketball/news/lebron-james-dream-3x3-team-jordan-magic-and-himself.

26. "IOC adds 3-on-3 basketball to 2020 Olympics." NBA.com. June 9, 2017. https://www.nba.com/news/ioc-votes-include-3-3-basketball-2020-tokyo-olympics.

27. "NBA Commissioner Adam Silver: '3x3 is incredibly exciting!'" FIBA 3x3. September 6, 2016. Video. https://www.youtube.com/watch?v=zWULFvdfT-E.

28. Vlad Ghizdareanu. Interview with author. June 29, 2020.

29. Brane Dežman. *Košarka za mlade igralce in igralke.* Ljubljana: Fakulteta za šport, Inštitut za šport, 2004.

30. "Authorized Access – Justise Winslow at Dew NBA 3X in Miami." NBA. June 19, 2017. Video. https://www.youtube.com/watch?v=7ml_lxNBAYM.

31. "Former NBA star Dennis Scott committed to help 3x3 grow in the U.S." FIBA. basketball. December 2, 2020. https://www.fiba.basketball/news/former-nba-star-dennis-scott-committed-to-help-3x3-grow-in-the-us.

32. "Here Comes 3x3: A Guide to Hosting." FIBA 3x3. PDF. https://fiba3x3.com/docs/FIBA-3x3-Guide-To-Hosting-Events.pdf.

33. Paul Montgomery and Brendan Maloney. "The Physical and Physiological Characteristics of 3x3: Results of Medical Study and Scientific Test." FIBA 3x3. PDF. https://fiba3x3.com/docs/fitness-requirements-of-3x3-players.pdf.